teach yourself

the british empire

teach®
yourself

the british empire
michael lynch

For over 60 years, more than
40 million people have learnt over
750 subjects the **teach yourself**
way, with impressive results.

be where you want to be
with **teach yourself**

For UK order enquiries: please contact Bookpoint Ltd, 130 Milton Park, Abingdon, Oxon OX14 4SB. Telephone: +44 (0) 1235 827720. Fax: +44 (0) 1235 400454. Lines are open 09.00–18.00, Monday to Saturday, with a 24-hour message answering service. Details about our titles and how to order are available at www.teachyourself.co.uk

For USA order enquiries: please contact McGraw-Hill Customer Services, PO Box 545, Blacklick, OH 43004-0545, USA. Telephone: 1-800-722-4726. Fax: 1-614-755-5645.

For Canada order enquiries: please contact McGraw-Hill Ryerson Ltd, 300 Water St, Whitby, Ontario L1N 9B6, Canada. Telephone: 905 430 5000. Fax: 905 430 5020.

Long renowned as the authoritative source for self-guided learning – with more than 40 million copies sold worldwide – the **teach yourself** series includes over 300 titles in the fields of languages, crafts, hobbies, business, computing and education.

British Library Cataloguing in Publication Data: a catalogue record for this title is available from the British Library.

Library of Congress Catalog Card Number: on file.

First published in UK 2005 by Hodder Education, 338 Euston Road, London, NW1 3BH.

First published in US 2005 by Contemporary Books, a Division of the McGraw-Hill Companies, 1 Prudential Plaza, 130 East Randolph Street, Chicago, IL 60601 USA.

This edition published 2005.

The **teach yourself** name is a registered trade mark of Hodder Headline.

Typeset by Transet Limited, Coventry, England.
Printed in Great Britain for Hodder Education, a division of Hodder Headline, 338 Euston Road, London NW1 3BH, by Cox & Wyman Ltd, Reading, Berkshire.

Hodder Headline's policy is to use papers that are natural, renewable and recyclable products and made from wood grown in sustainable forests. The logging and manufacturing processes are expected to conform to the environmental regulations of the country of origin.

Impression number   10 9 8 7 6 5 4 3 2 1
Year   2010 2009 2008 2007 2006 2005

contents

dedication

to ESL.

acknowledgements

The author wishes to make a special acknowledgement the following books:

The Dent Atlas of British History, Martin Gilbert, J.M. Dent, 1993.

The Dent Atlas of American History, Martin Gilbert, J.M. Dent, 1993.

01

the origins of the British empire

This chapter will cover:
- the scale and character of the empire
- the adventurers and explorers who created the early empire
- the growth of Britain's North American colonies.

Mad dogs and Englishmen

An appropriate place to start is with one of the wittiest and most instructive songs ever composed. Noël Coward's 'Mad Dogs and Englishmen' manages to convey the essence of the colonizers' air of superiority and the bewilderment of the colonized at the inability of the British to understand the constraints of local traditions and climate. It captures the confidence, the foolhardiness, the willingness to bear hardship of the British rulers and hints at concealed mockery of the rulers by the ruled. In addition it offers a lightning tour of the main parts of what was a vast empire on which the sun never set. It must be pointed out that Coward's song touches on only the tropical regions and even then leaves out Africa. It takes for granted the sheer physical range of the empire, an empire that included territory on every inhabited continent.

Even flat on the page, without Coward's extraordinary voice so redolent of imperial glories, and his impeccable timing, the song is a mini geography and history lesson.

> In tropical climes there are certain times of day
> When all the citizens retire
> To tear their clothes off and perspire.
> It's one of those rules that the greatest fools obey,
> Because the sun is much too sultry
> And one must avoid its ultry-violet ray.

> The natives grieve when the white men leave their huts,
> Because they're obviously definitely nuts!

> Mad dogs and Englishmen
> Go out in the midday sun,
> The Japanese don't care to.
> The Chinese wouldn't dare to,
> Hindoos and Argentines sleep firmly from twelve to one.
> But Englishmen detest a siesta.
> In the Philippines
> There are lovely screens
> To protect you from the glare.
> In the Malay States
> There are hats like plates
> Which the Britishers won't wear.
> At twelve noon
> The natives swoon

And no further work is done,
But mad dogs and Englishmen
Go out in the midday sun.

It's such a surprise for the Eastern eyes to see
That though the English are effete,
They're quite impervious to heat,
When the white man rides every native hides in glee,
Because the simple creatures hope he
Will impale his solar topee on a tree.

It seems such a shame
When the English claim
The earth
That they give rise to such hilarity and mirth.

Mad dogs and Englishmen
Go out in the midday sun.
The toughest Burmese bandit
Can never understand it.
In Rangoon the heat of noon
Is just what the natives shun.
They put their Scotch or Rye down
And lie down.
In a jungle town
Where the sun beats down
To the rage of man and beast
The English garb
Of the English sahib
Merely gets a bit more creased.
In Bangkok
At twelve o'clock
They foam at the mouth and run,
But mad dogs and Englishmen
Go out in the midday sun.

Mad dogs and Englishmen
Go out in the midday sun.
The smallest Malay rabbit
Deplores this foolish habit.
In Hong Kong
They strike a gong
And fire off a noonday gun

To reprimand each inmate
Who's in late.
In the mangrove swamps
Where the python romps
There is peace from twelve till two.
Even caribous
Lie around and snooze;
For there's nothing else to do.
In Bengal
To move at all
Is seldom, if ever done,
But mad dogs and Englishmen
Go out in the midday sun.

Source: The Complete Lyrics by Noël Coward. Methuen
Publishing Ltd. Copyright © The Estate of Noël Coward.

To start our tour of the British empire, let us examine each of
Coward's key references:

- **Japan** did not become part of the empire, but Britain did
  bring it into the modern world by imposing trade treaties on
  it in the nineteenth century. With great skill and adaptability,
  the Japanese copied western industrial and military patterns
  to turn themselves into a dominant force in Asia. After
  fighting as allies in the First World War, Britain and Japan
  were bitter enemies in the Second. It was Japan's crushing
  victories over her that helped to undermine Britain's
  confidence that she could maintain her empire east of Suez.

- Japan's neighbours, the **Chinese**, had a much less impressive
  record until 1945. Britain did not colonize China but in the
  nineteenth century she led the European powers in imposing
  a set of unequal treaties on the Chinese, which left much of
  their trade and many of their ports under foreign control.
  China came into the First World War on Britain's side in
  1917; this led to many thousands of Chinese serving as
  labourers on the Western Front. Four years after the Japanese
  invaded China in 1937, Britain joined the war as an ally of
  China. To show her good will during the struggle, Britain
  gave up all claim to special rights in China with the exception
  of Hong Kong; she also recruited many Chinese to serve as
  seamen in the British merchant fleet. Any hope that Britain
  might renew her dominance over China disappeared in 1949,
  the year the Chinese Communists under Mao Zedong took
  control of the country. Britain finally gave up Hong Kong in
  1997 on the expiry of a hundred year lease, signed in 1898.

- Reference to the **Hindoos** (more usually spelled as Hindus) points to the sub-continent of India, the 'jewel in the Crown', the most-prized of Britain's imperial possessions. Hinduism was one of the three major religions of the Indian people, the other two being Islam (Mohammedanism) and Sikhism, a faith that had broken away from Hinduism. The great religions were frequently in conflict, a complicating factor throughout modern Indian history which explains why, when independence from Britain came in 1947, the sub-continent was partitioned between Hindu India and Islamic Pakistan, which was further sub-divided into the two states of West and East Pakistan. The Sikhs remained an embittered third element who felt their rights had been ignored.

- There are parts of **Argentina** where Welsh is still spoken. This is a legacy of a nineteenth-century migration to South America of mine workers from Wales, Scotland and England. Argentina was never part of the British empire, but it had an important and sometimes chequered relationship with Britain. In 1828, for example, British naval strength was used to oblige the Argentines to give up their attempt to take over neighbouring Uruguay. But later in the century British investment helped considerably in the development of Argentina's railways. Britain also bought quality race horses and polo ponies from Argentina. With the development of ships with refrigerated holds, trade in quality flesh of another kind came with the large-scale importing of Argentinian beef into Britain. Fray Bentos was the best known variety of this. In 1982, in what was arguably the last great example of British imperialism in action, Britain retook the disputed Falklands Islands which had been occupied by Argentinian forces.

- The **Malay states** were a British Crown colony between 1867 and 1946. The British had made their first settlement on the Malay peninsula, a land rich in spices, rubber and oil, in 1786. During the following century the claiming of the key ports of Penang and Singapore led to all the main regions being brought under control. It was to be the loss of the Malay peninsula to the invading Japanese forces in 1942 that first raised the demanding question as to whether Britain was any longer physically capable of clinging on to her empire. The Malay states, after being defended against Communist insurgents by British troops during the Emergency of 1948–57, eventually gained independence as the new Malaysia in 1963.

- Coward's reference to the toughness of **Burmese bandits** was appropriate and accurate. For centuries Burma had been the home of lawless bands who refused to accept the authority of any form of central government. These brigands were among the most feared in Asia. Burma, a huge area of land lying between India and China and above Malaya, was of vital strategic importance to Britain as her empire expanded in the nineteenth century. Three wars were fought in 1826, 1852 and 1885 before British forces took control of it, and declared it to be part of British India. During the Second World War Burma was largely overrun by the Japanese, with Rangoon, the capital, and Mandalay both falling in 1942. The country became the scene of ferocious jungle fighting before the Japanese were finally defeated. A key role in this was played by a special force, who took the name Chindits after the fierce lion sculptures that were common in Burma. Led by the unorthodox but brilliant Orde Wingate, who died in action in 1944, the Chindits operated behind the Japanese lines constantly harassing and disrupting.

Coward, who composed his song in 1927, was writing of the British empire at its zenith in the twentieth century. What of its origins over four centuries earlier?

The early empire

'Vast honour is paid him and he goes dressed in silk and these English run after him like mad.' These words are from a letter by a foreign visitor describing the excitement aroused in England by the exploits of John Cabot, a Venetian explorer based in Bristol. If the expansion of England overseas can be said to have a specific beginning, the starting date would be 1497. In that year, Henry VII, the first Tudor monarch, had helped finance Cabot on an expedition to explore the coast of north America. His commission to Cabot read:

> John and his sons or their heirs and deputies may conquer, occupy and possess whatsoever such towns, castles, cities and islands by them thus discovered... acquiring for us the dominion, title and jurisdiction of the same towns, castle, cities, islands and mainlands so discovered.

The King's motives were not a simple love of adventure. He was much more hard-headed. Five years earlier, in 1492, Christopher Columbus had discovered central America and claimed the lands for Spain. Two years after that, in 1494, Spain and Portugal, with the Pope's approval, had signed a treaty claiming to divide the New World between them. To show his contempt for such arrogance, Henry urged Cabot to provide grounds for an English counter-claim in the Americas. Cabot obliged by crossing the Atlantic in his ship the *Matthew* and making a number of landings on the North American coast. In the soil of what later became the Canadian province of Newfoundland, he planted two flags. One was the Cross of St Mark, the patron saint of Venice; the other was the Cross of St George, the symbol of English authority. This was Britain's first tentative step towards acquiring an overseas empire. But neither Cabot nor Henry VII was aware of this. They could not know the extraordinary way in which that empire would develop over the next five centuries.

Although Cabot's success enlivened interest in exploration, there was no immediate effort to follow this up by creating overseas settlements. Henry's assertion of English rights had been essentially a gesture, a protest against the power of Spain and Portugal. As was so often the case throughout the history of the empire, little direction came from the top. When governments took action it was invariably in response to what had already happened.

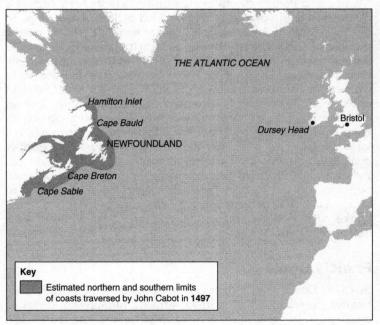

Figure 1 John Cabot's explorations

This was clearly the case in the 'golden age' of expansion – the reign of Elizabeth I (1558–1603). Britain's great Elizabethan heroes were the 'seadogs' such as John Hawkins, Francis Drake and Martin Frobisher. These men, whom the Queen ceremoniously elevated to knighthood, were pirates. They made their living by violently stealing other people's property, principally that of the Spaniards.

The English sea dogs and explorers

John Hawkins

John Hawkins came from a family of sailors who had become wealthy through a mixture of trade and piracy. One of the richest men in the west country, Hawkins had been a member of parliament in the reign of Henry VIII (1509–47). His special contribution to his country's overseas expansion was to introduce England to the benefits of the slave trade. Knowing that the Spanish needed workers to mine gold and silver in Mexico and Peru, a deadly underground activity for which few free men would volunteer, Hawkins led a fleet of five ships to the west coast of Africa in 1562. There he made contact with a number of tribal chiefs, offering to fight for them in their wars against neighbouring tribes on condition that instead of killing their prisoners, as was their usual custom, they handed them over to him. The chiefs agreed; the result was that Hawkins then sailed with hundreds of captured Africans for the Spanish colonies. Ignoring a Spanish law that prohibited non-Spaniards from trading in slaves, Hawkins sold his human cargo for a large profit. Two such slaving expeditions were successfully completed. However, on a third venture in 1567, the Spaniards cut up rough and tried to recover their money. Fighting broke out; some of the English crew were captured and tortured to death. Hawkins, accompanied by his young nephew, Francis Drake, managed to escape. They came home seething with hatred for Spain.

Francis Drake

In 1577, Drake with money advanced from some of the richer English merchants and with approval, though no financial backing, from the Queen, set out to sail round the world. His aim was not exploration for its own sake. He wanted to get his

own back on the Spaniards for cheating him over the slave-trading deal ten years earlier. Yet Drake himself was hardly faultless. In the intervening decade he had matured into a brilliant seaman and captain who used his skills to patrol the waters off Spain in order to seize the treasure ships that came back loaded with gold, silver, diamonds and sugar from the Americas. It was piracy, but since some of the captured money found its way through gifts and levies into the royal treasury, the practice had the blessing of Elizabeth and her government.

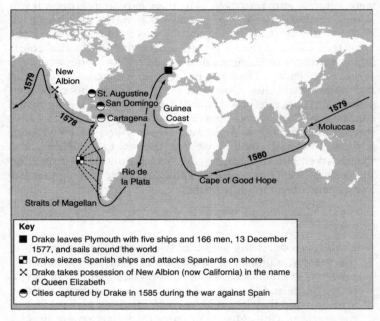

Figure 2 Drake's voyages

Whatever Drake's motives, and the modern age tends to judge him far more harshly than ever his English contemporaries did, the voyage itself was an extraordinary story of seamanship and courageous, if ruthless, determination. Starting from Plymouth, Drake sailed with five ships south across the Atlantic, through the Straits of Magellan into the Pacific, and then north up the coast of South America. His main targets were the Spanish treasure ships in the undefended ports of Chile and Peru. In a series of ferocious attacks he seized a huge amount of loot. One plundered vessel yielded up 12 chests of pieces of eight (the

English term for the Spanish silver dollar) and gold bars and nuggets weighing over 80 pounds. Drake's own ship, the *Golden Hind* was no longer ballasted with stones and clinkers but with gold and silver bullion.

The Spanish, whose bitter term for Drake was 'the dragon', sent out men-of-war to intercept his convoy as it sailed north after its raids, but he eluded them. Drake's hope was that he would discover a strait that would lead back into the Atlantic. Not finding one, he eventually reached California where his ships were refitted and restocked. He then explored further north hoping to find a north-west passage that might take him back into the Atlantic. Calculating that he was unlikely to escape the Spaniards a second time if he sailed back the way he had come, Drake made the momentous decision to sail for home westward across the Pacific. Putting in at the Moluccas islands in Indonesia, where they took on a cargo of spices, his ships then sailed south, rounded the Cape of Good Hope at the tip of the continent of Africa, and then north again. Eventually, in 1580, three years after he had set out, Drake sailed into Plymouth harbour. He had circumnavigated the world. The delighted Queen asked him to bring his ship to London. At Deptford, on the deck of the *Golden Hind*, Drake knelt to be knighted 'Sir Francis' by a beaming Elizabeth.

Drake's character and methods were described by a Spanish prisoner:

> Drake is of small size with a reddish beard, and is one of the greatest sailors that exist, both from his skill and power of commanding. He has a hundred men, all in the prime of life and well trained for war. He treats them with affection and they him with respect. He dines and sups to the music of viols. His ship carries thirty large guns, and a great quantity of ammunition, as well as workmen who can do necessary repairs.

Drake's astonishing voyage around the world reveals many features of the early empire: Anglo-Spanish rivalry, the extraordinary skill and daring of British seamen, and the eye for trade, plunder and profit. The backers who had helped finance Drake's adventure realised a return of 5,000 per cent on their original investment.

Drake did not sit back and indulge his fame and fortune. He continued to be a menace to Spanish shipping. His most outrageous exploit yet came in 1587 when, in English parlance, he 'singed the King of Spain's beard', by sailing into the port of Cadiz, sinking the ships moored there and blowing up all the store houses in the harbour. Among the supplies destroyed were the staves of seasoned wood used in ship repairs and in the making of barrels to hold water or gunpowder. The Spanish shipbuilders and coopers were reduced to working with unseasoned wood with the result that ships set sail with leaking seams and barrels that were liable to burst. This was to have fateful consequences a year later.

Spanish anger against Drake and his fellow English pirates for their State-backed, if not State-sponsored, terrorism led King Philip II to seek vengeance by launching an attempted invasion of England. In 1588, the Spanish Armada set sail only to be scattered in the English Channel by a combination of bad weather, poor tactics by the attackers and spirited resistance from the defenders. The lumbering Spanish galleons looked magnificent, but their lack of manoeuvrability made them easy targets for the English fire ships – unmanned boats loaded with gunpowder – which were set ablaze, and directed to drift into the Spanish fleet. A tale that Victorians later loved to tell has Drake waiting on Plymouth Ho for the Spanish and nonchalantly continuing with a game of bowls when told that the Armada had been sighted. Whether he actually said 'Let us finish our game' is less important than that the yarn neatly captures the essence of the man. He proceeded to patrol the Channel, forcing the Spanish ships to take harbour at Gravelines near Calais on the French coast. It was there that the fire boats inflicted their greatest damage.

Frobisher and the north-west passage

Many explorers around this time were inspired by the desire to find 'a north-west passage'. Now fully aware that that the world was round, explorers were intrigued as to whether by sailing west they could eventually reach the east. What prevented this was the American continent. The hope, therefore, was that there was a strait or opening waiting to be discovered that would allow ships through. Much of the transatlantic exploration had this as an objective. At about the same time as Drake was on his startling circumnavigation, another Englishman, Martin Frobisher, was seeking the elusive passage. Believing America to be a giant island that it was possible to sail round, Frobisher in his ship *Gabriel* made three voyages between 1576 and 1578. He reached what became known as Frobisher Bay and then sailed some 150 miles westwards along the northern coast of Baffin island, thinking that he had reached Asia. He had not, nor had he discovered the passage he dreamed of, but he had added hugely to the world's knowledge of the northern seas and lands.

Henry Hudson

England's explorers and adventurers aroused the resentment of the other seafaring nations of Europe – Holland, Spain, France and Portugal. Yet, in the midst of the growing rivalry, there were times of co-operation. In 1609 the Dutch East India Company, seeking a shorter and cheaper route to Asia other than by going round the Cape of Good Hope, commissioned Henry Hudson, an Englishman, to lead an expedition to look for a northern passage. Hudson, who had learned a great deal about northern waters as a member of the Muscovy Company which traded with Russia, set sail from Amsterdam in a ship provide by the Dutch, the 80-ton *Half Moon*. It carried a crew of 20 men drawn from both England and Holland.

Hudson intended first to look for a north-east passage, but after a troublesome journey along the coast of Norway during which the crew threatened to mutiny, Hudson turned west to America. After exploring Chesapeake and Hudson Bays in the hope that they might lead to a strait, he went north and turned into New York Bay. He then sailed up the river, which now bears his name, as far as Albany before realizing yet again that there was no way through. Hudson's own term for the waterway he had discovered was 'River of Mountains'. He described the region as 'as pleasant a land as one can tread upon'.

After both trading and fighting with the Indians near an island called Manhattan, the expedition sailed back across the Atlantic, reaching Dartmouth after a total journey of nine months. Here Hudson parted company with his Dutch employers; he stayed in England while the *Half Moon*, with its Dutch sailors, returned to Holland. Undaunted by having failed to find a passage, Hudson agreed a year later to lead a further expedition, this time funded by a group of London merchants. As captain of the *Discovery*, he set out in the summer of 1610. After stopping off in Iceland for a brief period, he sailed by the tip of Greenland, into the Hudson Strait and then turned south into the vast area of Hudson Bay, eventually making landfall in James Bay. These, of course, were all names that were given later to his discoveries. It was in James Bay that his ship became trapped in the ice, obliging him to remain there for the winter of

1610–11. By the time the spring thaw came, food had run low and the crew had mutinied. Hudson, his son, and four other loyal crew members, were cast adrift in an open boat. They were never seen again and their remains were never recovered. Whatever Hudson's faults may have been, and he seems to have had a knack of upsetting his crews, it was a tragic and unfitting end for a man whose daring ventures, like Frobisher's, had done so much to increase understanding of the northern hemisphere.

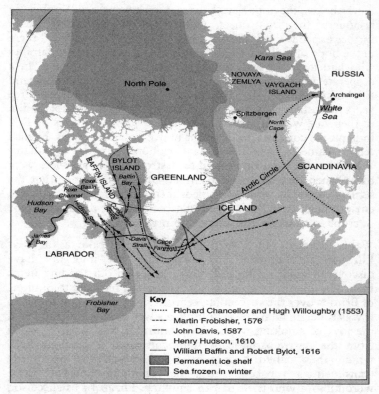

Figure 3 voyages of Frobisher and Hudson

Early attempts at settlement – Raleigh and Virginia

Drake had made no attempt to occupy the territories he landed on. The first genuine effort at English settlement came five years after Drake's voyage and it ended in disaster. Queen Elizabeth, not wishing to antagonize Spain unduly, had agreed to restrict English exploration of the Americas to the areas north of the Spanish possession of Florida. In 1585 Walter Raleigh led a party to Roanoke island. His aim was not permanent settlement what he had in mind was the setting up of a base for explorations further into America to find the gold that he and many Englishmen of the time believed was there in abundance. The dream proved false. There was no gold. Raleigh sailed home.

Nevertheless, the hope that the area, which he named 'Virginia' in honour of the virgin queen, might yield up other riches led to further expeditions to the area. In 1587 John White landed there in the hope of making it habitable for a group of English families who had travelled with him. They had a hard time of it. In a desperate attempt to save his people White sailed back to England to obtain fresh supplies. However, by the time he returned three years later there was no trace of them. The likeliest explanation of their fate was that they had been carried off as slaves by Red Indians, the colonists' term for the native American tribes. English settlers came to have a love–hate relationship with the Indians. While the two sides often tried to destroy each other, there were times when they co-operated. Much of the knowledge that the settlers acquired which enabled them to survive in a harsh environment came from the Indians who taught them what type of crops to cultivate and animals to rear.

Walter Raleigh ranks with Hawkins and Drake as a great Elizabethan buccaneer and adventurer. He may not have discovered gold but he did bring back two outstanding items from Virginia that were to bring benefit and pleasure to millions of Britons over the succeeding centuries – potatoes and tobacco. It was Raleigh, who himself puffed a silver pipe, who introduced the joys of smoking to the royal court. It was an art learned from the native Americans who cultivated a precious herb which they called 'uppowoc', and which the Spaniards translated as 'tobacco'. From the beginning, however, there were killjoys who tried to ban smoking. Elizabeth I's successor, James I (1603–25) condemned it as a 'barbarous and beastly' habit, fit only for 'the godless and slavish Indians'. He changed his mind, however, when, caught in a thunderstorm while out hunting, he took shelter in a pig-sty. Finding the foul smell too much to bear, he ordered his attendants to light up their pipes.

Raleigh died as dramatically as his lived. Condemned on a trumped up charge, he was executed in 1618 on the King's orders as part of a policy to appease Spain with whom James was trying to develop better relations. Raleigh behaved with characteristic dignity on the scaffold. Declining to be blindfolded, he asked the crowd who had come to see him beheaded to pray for him and to remember him as 'a seafaring man, a soldier and a courtier'. One of the consequences of his remarkable life was the quickening of England's interest in overseas territories both as sources of profit and places of settlement.

Despite the disaster of the first venture, another attempt was made to settle Virginia in 1606. James I granted a royal charter to a company specially formed to develop the area. A group of 105 people made their way to Chesapeake Bay and created a settlement known as Jamestown. Within a year, hardship and disease had reduced their number to 32, but these hardy souls persevered. They were joined in 1608 by Captain John Smith whose toughness as a leader helped save the colony. Elected president of the local council in September 1608, he demanded strict discipline from the colonists, warning them that only by their own efforts could they survive. His watchword was: 'He who will not work, neither shall he eat.' Smith also made sincere attempts to get on good terms with the surrounding native tribes, joining in their rituals and learning their language. It was Smith who first befriended the young Algonquian princess Pocahontas after she had interceded for him when she mistakenly thought her father intended killing him. Pocahontas, whose name means 'playful little girl' later married an Englishman and went to live in London where she became something of a celebrity. There is a monument to her in St George's Church in Gravesend in Kent, recording that she had been buried there in 1617, having died at the age of 22.

Encouraged by the colonists' determination, the Virginia Company raised more capital and offered those who chose to settle full ownership of the land instead of merely tenant rights. The offer worked; by 1622 there were 1,500 people in the colony. However, in that year things rapidly changed. An Indian attack wiped out 350 of the settlers in the remoter regions. On top of that, the Virginia Company, unable to pay a dividend to its shareholders, was wound up in 1624. Things looked bleak for the Virginians. Salvation came in the form of a government takeover. The Crown declared itself to be the owner of the colony. To regularize the new position a permanent Governor was sent to Virginia to act on the King's behalf. His chief task was to oversee the colony's trade and internal affairs. But, in an interesting move, the colonists were granted an elected assembly which had a considerable say in domestic matters.

New England

The principal motive in the establishing of Virginia had been a commercial one. Quite another purpose inspired the creation of a number of colonies north of Virginia. A group of believers known for the strictness of their faith as 'Puritans' – they wished to 'purify' worship of all unnecessary rituals – decided to leave England and settle in America. Their aim was to create a religious community free of the control of the Anglican Church whose doctrines they rejected. In 1620, together with a number of merchants, these 'Pilgrim fathers' led by Miles Standish and William Bradford, set sail across the Atlantic in the *Mayflower*. After 67 days at sea, they made landfall in Massachusetts Bay at a place they named Plymouth. There they began creating 'a city on a hill', their term for a settlement based on religious principles and observance.

What began in 1620 as a small village had grown by 1643 into a large town of 25,000 people, many of the newcomers being religious refugees from England where anti-Puritan persecution had been intensified under Charles I (1625–49). Life was hard for the colonists. The soil and climate did not make for easy farming; famine was a constant threat. This was why the settlers turned for their livelihood to the sea for cod fishing and whaling and to the forests for shipbuilding. A combination of burning religious conviction, sheer hard work, and a realistic grasp of basic economics saw Massachusetts and the other colonies of the area, known as New England, survive and begin to prosper.

Maryland

One concept of religious freedom inspired the setting up of the New England colonies; another lay behind the founding of Maryland. In 1632, Charles I accepted a petition from Lord Baltimore asking for permission to establish an American colony where Catholics would be free to practise their faith. Two years later, the first group of Catholics sailed into Chesapeake Bay and then up the Potomac River to a base called St Mary's, around which they began to construct a new settlement. As a mark of loyalty and gratitude to the King's Catholic wife, Henrietta Maria, they christened the new colony, Maryland. As in Virginia, its neighbour state, Maryland began to build a successful economy mainly on the growing and selling of tobacco. This led, by the end of the seventeenth century, to an increasing reliance on black slave labour, brought from west Africa, to work the large plantations on which the tobacco was grown.

Different types of settlement

The founding of Maryland and New England offers a good illustration of the two main types of colony in British North America. Maryland is an example of a 'proprietary colony' where a wealthy person obtained a royal patent or grant giving him control over a certain area which he then invited people to live on as his tenants. However, the New England states – Connecticut, Massachusetts (which included Plymouth), New Hampshire, and Rhode Island – are examples of 'corporate colonies'; the term refers to the way in which a number of people with a special interest created and settled a colony and then applied for a royal charter recognizing their right to run the area as they chose. Each type of colony accepted that its ultimate allegiance was to the King and his Parliament.

It was along one or other of these lines that the 13 colonies that were ultimately to form the USA came into being in just over a century between 1624–1732. A notable feature of most of the settlements was that no matter what the reasons for their origins had been – to escape religious persecution or poverty or to gain economic and political freedom – they quickly began to exploit the local conditions to develop strong economies. Few of the colonies were content to remain at subsistence level; they wanted to trade and grow rich. Carolina is an interesting example. Founded as a proprietary colony in 1663, it lay between Virginia to the north and Spanish Florida to the south. The hope of its original founders, who included such eminent figures as George Monck, the general who more than anyone was responsible for restoring Charles II to his throne in 1660, was that it would provide England with silks, fruit and oil that previously had to be bought from Mediterranean countries. But while it did provide these things, its wealth came from its sale of rice and cotton, crops which flourished in its frost-free climate and which were eagerly bought by Europe.

England's colonizing did not go unchallenged. France and Holland also held territories in North America. The French had established themselves along the St Lawrence River and around the lower Mississippi. They had also taken territories in the

Caribbean. The Dutch had founded New Amsterdam (later to
be New York) at the mouth of the Hudson River which linked
them with the St Lawrence River and Canada. In addition, they
had occupied land around the Delaware River, a region between
the New England states and Virginia. There was every chance
that the continent would become a theatre of war between the
competing European imperial powers.

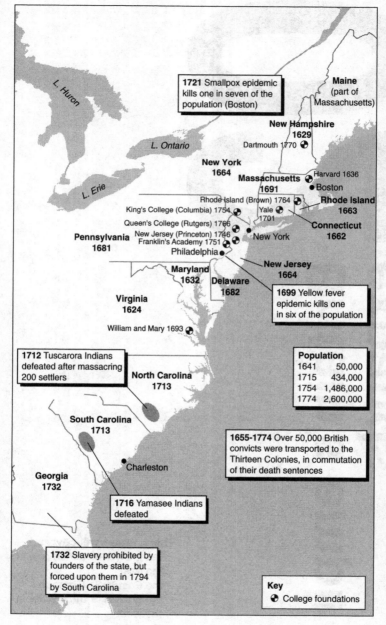

1721 Smallpox epidemic kills one in seven of the population (Boston)

Maine (part of Massachusetts)

New Hampshire 1629

Dartmouth 1770 ◑

L. Huron

L. Ontario

L. Erie

New York 1664

Massachusetts 1691

Harvard 1636 ◑

Boston

Rhode Island (Brown) 1764 ◑

King's College (Columbia) 1754 ◑

Yale ◑ 1701

Rhode Island 1663

Queen's College (Rutgers) 1766 ◑

Connecticut 1662

Pennsylvania 1681

New Jersey (Princeton) 1746 ◑

Franklin's Academy 1751 ◑

New York

Philadelphia ●

Maryland 1632

Delaware 1682

New Jersey 1664

Virginia 1624

1699 Yellow fever epidemic kills one in six of the population

William and Mary 1693 ◑

Population

1641	50,000
1715	434,000
1754	1,486,000
1774	2,600,000

1712 Tuscarora Indians defeated after massacring 200 settlers

North Carolina 1713

South Carolina 1713

1655-1774 Over 50,000 British convicts were transported to the Thirteen Colonies, in commutation of their death sentences

Charleston

Georgia 1732

1716 Yamasee Indians defeated

1732 Slavery prohibited by founders of the state, but forced upon them in 1794 by South Carolina

Key
◑ College foundations

Figure 4 the 13 British colonies in North America

02

Britain's empire expands

This chapter will cover::
- the growth of the empire in the east
- the East India Company
- the growth of the empire in the west
- slavery.

Expansion in the East

The spice trade

Strained though Britain's relations were with the Dutch in America, it was in a very different part of the world that Anglo-Dutch rivalry was at its sharpest. Holland's powerful navy had allowed her to seize many of the areas in the East Indies originally set up by the Spanish and Portuguese in Indonesia and the Philippines. By the start of the seventeenth century the Dutch East India Company had gained a monopoly over the trade in cloth and spices.

The intense competition for the spice trade is easy to understand. Huge profits could be made. In 1620, a quarter of a million pounds of pepper bought for £26,000 in the East Indies, fetched £208,333 when sold in London. Similarly, cloves bought for £5,126, sold for £45,000. Such spices were not merely a way of adding taste to food – they acted as preservatives. Before the days of refrigeration, which did not come in until the late nineteenth century, meat could not be easily stopped from rotting. Salt was the main method of preservation, but this often left the meat hard and unpalatable. Spices, however, could both preserve food and give it piquancy. The trade in spice became a major industry and directly connected Britain to a whole variety of areas overseas:

- Pepper from India and Ceylon (later Sri Lanka)
- Cardamom from Ceylon
- Nutmeg and cloves from the Moluccas islands
- Fenugreek from China and India
- Aniseed from the eastern Mediterranean
- Vanilla from the West Indies and Central America
- Turmeric from tropical Asia
- Chilli from South America.

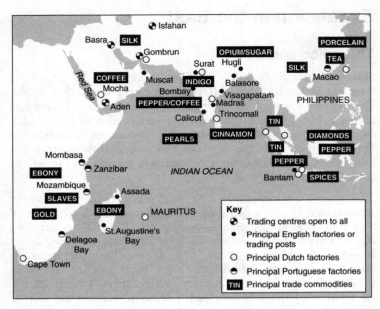

Figure 5 the areas from which the spices and other commodities came

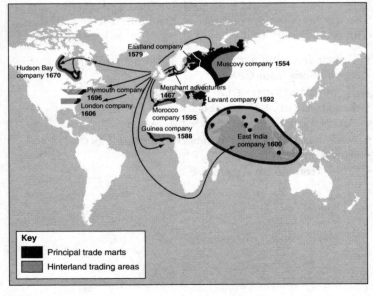

Figure 6 British trading companies

The English East India Company (EEIC)

In an attempt to rival the Dutch, a group of English merchants, particularly outraged by a rise in 1599 in the price of pepper from 3 shillings (15p) to 8 shillings (40p) a pound, set up an English East India Company. Some 200 investors contributed £70,000 (roughly equivalent to £2 million in today's values) to form the Company.

In January 1600, Elizabeth I granted the EEIC a charter, giving it the sole right to trade in 'the East Indies, in the countries and Parts of Asia and Africa, and into and from all the islands, Ports, Havens, Cities, Creeks, Towns and Places in Asia, Africa, and America, or any of them beyond the Cape of Bona Esperanza [Good Hope]'. With the trade monopoly went the right to raise taxes and own and dispose of land in any areas which the Company occupied. These were extensive powers and in time the EEIC was to use them to build the largest single organization and provider of employment in the empire's history. The Company would develop its own administration, legal system and army and would amass huge wealth for its shareholders.

Yet the EEIC's beginnings were not promising. When it tried to break into the Indonesian spice trade, the Dutch forced the growers to stop selling to the English. In 1623, on the island of Amboyna, 18 British merchants were tortured before being slaughtered by Dutch troops. The Company did not totally abandon the spice trade but, concentrating on India, turned instead to cottons and silks. Spices had attracted the EEIC to Asia; quality fabrics were the reason why it stayed.

The Company already had a base in India. At this time the Indian sub-continent was ruled by the Mogul Emperor in Delhi. Under him were a number of princes. They acknowledged the Emperor's sovereignty and paid tribute to him, but they were lords in their own separate provinces, collecting taxes and maintaining law and order. The Emperor had allowed a ship to land at Surat on the western coast in 1608. Six years later, following a mission by an English ambassador, Sir Thomas Rowe, to the Mogul court, Emperor Jahangir granted the Company a 'farman' (a royal charter), permitting the EEIC to establish a permanent settlement and giving it official trading rights and protection.

By 1650, the English East India Company had 23 sites in Calcutta, Madras and Bombay. Trade began to flourish. In 1675 the Company sent £800,000 worth of Indian cloth to Britain in exchange for British manufactured goods. The materials from India created a revolution in English fashion. Cotton, muslin, taffeta, chintz, calico (the word refers to Calcutta) and silk provided the clothing for the British people and the hangings in the British home from the seventeenth century until the development of synthetic fibres in the twentieth.

The Company also extended its trade as far as China. Fine porcelain from there began to adorn the tables of the fashionable in London. Equally significantly, the goods were shipped in Company-owned vessels. Competition with rival powers meant that the Company's ships had to be armed. Most East India merchantmen, as the ships were known, carried at least one cannon. But it was still expected that the Royal Navy would defend British vessels on the high seas and in port against foreign ships and pirates. The problem was that in the early seventeenth century Britain's navy was in a very rough and ready state of development.

The difficulty was two-fold – lack of a permanent navy and lack of warships. As with soldiers on land, men were enlisted for naval duties or pressed into service only when there was a war. There was no professional army or navy. Similarly, there was no fleet of warships kept ready for action. It is true that Henry VIII had been famed for the quality of the warships he had had constructed. The *Mary Rose* (recovered from the sea bed almost intact in 1982) and the *Great Harry* had been admired throughout Europe. But these were but two of a handful of purpose-built craft, which in any case were out of commission in peacetime. In an emergency, as had been shown at the time of the Armada in 1588, when a mixture of luck and skilful English seamanship destroyed the Spanish invasion, all and any sort of ships available had to be relied on.

Technically, the Company was under the direct control of its London headquarters, but in practice it was independent and a law unto itself. This was not out of disloyalty or defiance of authority. It arose from the difficulty of maintaining contact. While it took only six weeks to reach America from England, it took six months to travel from Britain to India and the same for the return journey. It was not simply a matter of distance; what added to the time was waiting for the prevailing winds which blew in the required east or west direction for only half the year. Twelve months were needed, therefore, to send an instruction or request and receive a reply. The result was that day-to-day decisions had to be made in India itself, giving increasing power to the Company's officials (or 'servants' as they were called). What was equally interesting was that a form of partnership and co-operation developed between the Company and the Indian people, large numbers of whom became workers in the warehouses, offices, docks and harbours (known collectively as factories) that the Company set up. A crucial fact was that the Company's existence in India depended on the good will of the Emperor and the princes. They allowed the EEIC to continue to trade in return for substantial payments of tax. There was thus a shared wish among the Indians and the English residents to see the Company prosper.

By the end of the seventeenth century the EEIC was a major force in international trade. However, it is worth stressing that at this time India was a great trading nation in its own right. Important though the EEIC was in the growth of Britain's empire, the Company's activities made up only a relatively small part of India's business. An example of this is that the Company sent out on average only one shipload of goods each month. By far the larger proportion of Indian trade went overland, by caravan, into Central Asia. At the beginning of the eighteenth century, the Mogul empire out-produced and out-sold all the states of Europe put together. In 1700, India had 24 per cent of the world's trade, compared to Britain's 3 per cent.

Thomas 'Diamond' Pitt – a nabob

The detachment of the EEIC from direct control provided opportunities for individuals to grow rich by using its contacts. One such was Thomas Pitt. Described by the Company whom he fell out with as 'a desperate young fellow of a haughty, huffing, daring temper' who would not hesitate to perform 'any mischief that lay within his power', Pitt was what might be called today a wheeler-dealer or a hustler. Born into a religious family in Dorset, he left England in 1673 to take up an EEIC post in India. Before long, he had begun to trade on his own behalf, exploiting the Company's supplies and accounting system to make private deals with local traders. He bought goods on the cheap and sent them back for sale in England. Angered at being undercut by one of their own employees, the Company tried to dismiss him and send him back home. Pitt outflanked them by doing a deal with Matthias Vincent, the Company's chief executive in Madras, and then marrying Vincent's niece. When the Company continued to chase him, he made an out-of-court settlement with them to the tune of £400, which was a mere fraction of what he had amassed.

Pitt stayed on in India building up his private empire. Such was his energy and ability as an entrepreneur, that the Company swallowed its pride and offered him the post of Governor of Fort St George in Madras. Pitt accepted. It gave him a perfect base for increasing his own fortune. However, he did not have an entirely easy time as Governor. He had to defend the fort against an attack by a local nawab (prince). The nawab was carrying out the wishes of the Mogul Emperor Aurungzeb who, temporarily at least, had withdrawn his permission for the Company to trade in India. Pitt succeeded in negotiating a satisfactory settlement, and business returned to normal. But the incident had revealed that, powerful though the Company appeared to have become, its existence ultimately depended on the good will of the Emperor and the nawabs.

The term 'nawab' is one of the many words that were borrowed from Indian dialects and became a permanent part of English vocabulary; other examples are: bungalow, veranda, pyjamas, blighty and khaki. However, with 'nawab' an interesting semantic shift occurred. Whereas the original word denoted an Indian prince, in its anglicized form 'nabob' referred to those English entrepreneurs, like Pitt, who made themselves very rich from their dealings in India. While it is true that English invariably became the dominant language in the lands of the empire it was not completely one-way traffic.

As with most of the nabobs who followed him, Thomas Pitt became renowned for flaunting his wealth. The nineteenth century writer and historian, Lord Macaulay, said that the nabobs 'raised the price of everything in their neighbourhood from fresh eggs to rotten boroughs'. Pitt ploughed much of his money into properties back home in England, buying the Boconnoc estate in Cornwall as a family seat. His most ostentatious display was to buy what became known as the Pitt Diamond. Cut from the Mogul's mines, the 410 carat gem was valued at £125,000, truly priceless by today's standards. Pitt later sold it at a profit to the French Duke of Orléans. The giant diamond then became one of the jewels in the French crown from where Napoleon extracted it to place it in the hilt of one of his ceremonial swords. It now resides in the Louvre in Paris.

The fierce rivalry between the English and Dutch East India Companies effectively came to an end in the 1690s. This was not a case of one side's overcoming the other in India. It was a product of English politics. In the 'Glorious Revolution' of

1688–9, the Catholic King James II abdicated to be replaced by Parliament's nominee, William III. Since the new king was both Dutch and Protestant, this helped create a harmony of commercial interests. A number of Dutchmen joined the board of the East India Company. This amounted to a merger between the two companies, from which Britain gained greatly since she could now call upon the more advanced banking and financial skills which the Dutch had developed. One example of this was the creation of the Bank of England in 1694, an institution that was to be an indispensable support to all British governments from that time on.

Religion and trade

It is important to understand the part religion played in shaping England's early attitude towards the empire. The Reformation, which had begun in the reign of Henry VIII (1509–47) and had been completed under his daughter, Elizabeth I (1553–1603), had made England a Protestant nation. This put her at loggerheads with Catholic Spain whose Habsburg rulers believed it was their religious duty to lead a crusade against countries such as England, which had rejected the true Catholic faith. The unsuccessful attempt of the Armada to invade England in 1588 was the outstanding example of Anglo-Spanish hostility. For over a century after, distrust of Spain remained a dominant English attitude, particularly among Puritans – the more extreme form of Protestants. They wanted England to head an alliance of the European Protestant nations against Spain. Little came of this during the reigns of the early Stuarts (1603–49), since both James I and Charles I chose to avoid foreign entanglements where possible.

No foreign country played a direct part in the English civil wars between King and Parliament in the years 1642–51. One reason was that Europe was largely preoccupied with the last stages of the Thirty Years War, which occurred between 1618 and 1648.

This had started as a struggle between Catholic and Protestant states, but as the war progressed it became increasingly difficult to define it in religious terms. In fact in 1635 the two major Catholic powers, Spain and France, went to war against each other.

It was this blurring of the religious issue that explains why foreign alignments no longer formed simply along lines of religious faith; other considerations began to influence national attitudes. Foremost among these was economics. For more than a century, trade rivalry in Europe and overseas had been a cause of growing hostility between England and other continental countries. Where religious division and commercial rivalry coincided, as with England and Spain, mutual dislike was the logical outcome. But it was seldom as simple as that. Religious sympathies and commercial interests did not always match. Such was the case with England and Holland. Although the two countries shared a common Protestantism, this did not create a harmony of interest. Their trade rivalry in Europe and the East Indies became more important than their religious sympathies. This became clearly apparent with the ending of the Thirty Years War in 1648, which had the disturbing result for England of leaving the large Dutch merchant fleet free to monopolize the shipping routes in the North Sea and the Baltic.

This worried the merchant-dominated English Parliament, known as the Rump, which ruled England following the execution of Charles I in 1649. At first it tried to reach an agreement with the Dutch, but talks broke down. The Rump's leading ambassador, Oliver St John, condemned the Dutch for being concerned solely with their own self-interest. He described them as 'juggling sharks'. At his suggestion, the Rump introduced a Navigation Act in 1651 (renewed in 1660) as a way of punishing the Dutch for their refusal to consider an alliance and their aggressive trading methods.

The Navigation Act

The passing of the Act was a critical moment in imperial history. It stipulated that all goods imported into Britain from Africa, Asia or the Americas were to be carried only in British vessels, and that goods from Europe were to be admitted into Britain only in British ships or those of the exporting country. No third party trading was to be allowed. The Act is an early example of mercantilism, a form of protection or trade war. The introduction of the Navigation Act was accompanied by the deliberate whipping up of anti-Dutch hysteria. The Rump encouraged the publication of cheap newspapers and broadsheets depicting the Dutch as renegade Protestants corrupted by thoughts of commercial gain. The Dutch retaliated by denouncing what they regarded as English fanaticism and hypocrisy. Open war between the countries broke out in the early 1650s.

Oliver Cromwell

Moves towards peace were hastened by the coming to power in 1653 of Oliver Cromwell as Lord Protector, who was effectively the uncrowned king of England until his death in 1658. Cromwell had been a reluctant supporter of war against Holland. He regarded it as a scandal that Englishmen should be fighting fellow-Protestants. His abiding conviction was that Spain was still the great threat. He was fond of remarking that 'the Spaniard is your natural enemy'. Cromwell believed that he was singled out by God to fight the forces of Anti-Christ, whom he identified in Europe as the Spanish. One way to achieve this would be to unite the Protestant nations of Europe in a godly mission to chastise Spain.

The outcome was a peace treaty, signed in April 1654, under which the Dutch agreed to abide by the Navigation Act and to respect the English fleet at sea. Complaints were voiced in England that the Protector had failed to reap greater commercial gains from the peace settlement and it was certainly true that Cromwell at this stage was much more concerned with promoting an anti-Spanish alliance with the Dutch than with enforcing harsh economic terms on them. He was even prepared to offer the Dutch a monopoly of the East India trade if they would wage war on Spain.

A contemporary royalist historian, the Earl of Clarendon, famously wrote that England under Cromwell during the Protectorate was held in awe and fear by continental Europe. It is also true that the policies followed by Cromwell in this period went far beyond his time in their significance. Britain's later development as an empire could not have occurred in the way that it did but for his achievements in foreign affairs.

The Western Design

The defeat of the Dutch encouraged other European nations to enter into trade agreements with England. This strengthened Cromwell's determination to challenge the power of Spain. The area chosen for attack was the Spanish colonies in the Americas, hence the later description of it as 'the Western Design'. The essential aim was to capture the Spanish-controlled Caribbean islands and then turn them into permanent bases from which the English could destroy Spain's fleets and so break her empire.

The decision to attack Spain was taken in the weeks immediately following the end of the Dutch war in April 1654, which had left England with 150 war ships and their crews available. Cromwell denounced the King of Spain as 'the greatest enemy to the Protestant cause in the world' and argued that England had every right to retaliate for the wrongs done to her people. He said to Parliament:

> ... How empty and weak the reasons are that the Spaniard has for claiming for himself alone an empire of such vast and prodigious extent. The Spaniards endeavour to justify themselves for having enslaved, hanged, drowned, tortured and put to death our countrymen, robbed them of their ships and goods even in time of profound peace.

Not all the English merchants were eager for war. This was because they represented a range of commercial interests. Some merchants stood to gain greatly from the English seizure of Spain's territories and the takeover of its trade. Others, such as the wool merchants who traded directly with Spain, were unhappy at the prospect of a war that would bring trade disruption. It was out of deference to this latter group that the decision was made to restrict the war to an attack upon the Spanish colonies and to leave European Spain untouched.

As with the Dutch war, the prelude to war against Spain was a full-scale propaganda campaign. The enemy was depicted as a ravening beast, intent on destroying Protestant liberties and imposing the 'universal tyranny' of Spain over the whole world. A torrent of illustrated pamphlets invoked folk memories of the Armada and the Inquisition.

Indeed, greater planning seems to have gone into preparing public opinion for the war than into the attack on the Spanish colonies. The broad strategy was clear enough. The large fleet that set sail in December 1654, commanded by William Penn, the father of the Quaker who was later to found the American colony of Pennsylvania, aimed to capture the main Spanish-occupied islands in the Caribbean, Hispaniola (modern Haiti) being the principal target. Britain already occupied the islands of St Kitts, Barbados, Nevis, Montserrat and Antigua.

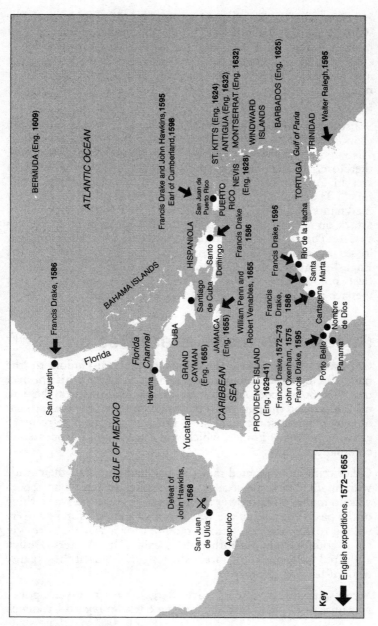

Figure 7 British expansion in the Caribbean

However, the tactics adopted were not well-thought out. The wrong area of the island was chosen for landing, distances were miscalculated, and the troops were struck down by a combination of extreme heat and disease. Spanish resistance also proved very determined. The English had to withdraw. Very much as an afterthought, they redirected their forces into what proved to be a successful attack upon Jamaica.

Subsequent history was to show that, strategically and economically, the island of Jamaica was as valuable a prize as Hispaniola would have been. Its capture could be said, therefore, to have fulfilled the chief purpose of the Western Design. At the time, however, it seemed that the campaign had failed. Thousands of troops had been lost. In addition, as many merchants had feared, Spain had retaliated to the unprovoked attack on her colonies by closing her European ports to English vessels. The Dutch were prompt to make up for their recent war losses by moving into the trading areas now barred to the English. Another unintended result was that, with the English fleet preoccupied in the Caribbean, piracy, an ever-present menace in this period, had a free hand elsewhere.

Reaction to the Western Design

Cromwell, who ascribed the failure to take Hispaniola to 'the hand of God', found himself the subject of fierce criticism over the war. Some complained that in his religious zeal he had misunderstood the nature of 'universal tyranny', the main threat of which came, some suggested, not from Spain but from the growing power of France, which was intent upon European and colonial domination.

Other critics complained that the war had damaged their trade with Spain. They saw it as an unnecessary struggle since Spain was no longer a real power in Europe; her greatness was a thing of the past. The cost of the war was also a key factor. Few were willing to pay the heavy taxes required for a war that brought them commercial loss rather than gain. The Western Design appeared to be pursuing unrealistic religious ends at the expense of hard-headed commercial ones.

Yet in spite of the contemporary charges that Cromwell's policy was unrealistic, it is possible, looking back, to regard Cromwell as a founder of the British empire. His Western Design laid stress on the gaining and settling of colonies and bases from which a trading empire could be spread. He also encouraged the English colonists in North America to expand into neighbouring regions belonging to Holland and France. One example was his dispatch of a naval squadron to seize Acadia (modern Nova Scotia) from the French in 1654. Equally significantly, Cromwell was keen to support English emigration to the West Indian islands. It became official Protectorate policy to promote settlement in Jamaica. Assisted passages and land were offered as incentives.

There was no great rush to take up such offers. The only settlers who went in any numbers to Jamaica and the other islands in the 1650s were prisoners sentenced to transportation, and young orphans sent as indentured apprentices. Nevertheless, the policy established a vital precedent. For the first time in English history, central government had undertaken the responsibility of promoting organized overseas settlement, rather than leave it as a matter of individual or group enterprise. Thus the basis for imperial expansion had been laid.

Slavery

The West Indian islands quickly developed as centres of sugar production, responding to an ever-growing European demand. By 1684 there were nearly 250 large plantations in Jamaica alone. This development could not have occurred without the availability of slaves. The cultivation and gathering of the sugar crop was an arduous and very labour intensive activity. There were simply not enough native islanders or free settlers to perform it. The only solution was the importation of slaves. This began a process known as the triangular trade. Slaves from the Ivory and Gold Coasts of West Africa were shipped to the West Indies or to the southern colonies of America where they were exchanged for commodities such as sugar, cotton, or tobacco which were then taken to Britain for sale. The third line of the triangle from Britain to West Africa involved conveying cheap goods, trinkets and iron bars which the African chiefs took as a form of exchange when selling their people into slavery, thus restarting the whole pattern.

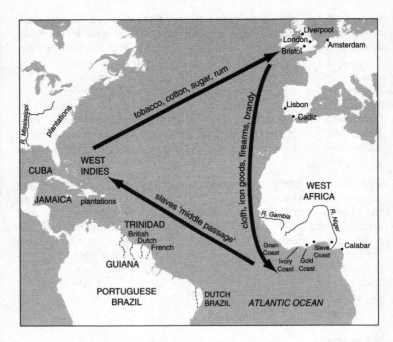

Figure 8 the triangular trade

Perhaps the worst part of this unremittingly brutal process was the second leg of the journey, 'the middle passage'. Packed into holds below decks, denied fresh air or sanitation, the bewildered, disorientated slaves suffered appallingly during the long crossing which took several weeks. Since life was so cheap, the traders took little effort to treat the slaves as valuable cargo. Deaths, many from suicide, were frequent. Calculations were that if 60 per cent survived the passage, it would be enough to guarantee a worthwhile profit when the slaves were sold off on reaching their destination.

It has been reckoned that between 1640 and 1807 as many as three million African captives may have been sold into slavery by British traders. The dismal reflection is that few nations or peoples come well out of the story of slavery. The truth is that slavery already existed in Africa long before the Europeans came. Indeed, Europe was itself a prey to slavery in the seventeenth and eighteenth centuries; during that period, the Islamic Barbary pirates roamed from Greece to Iceland, seizing some one million captives for sale in the slave markets of Morocco and Algeria. Several raids were made on the Cornish coast.

In Africa it was common practice during the frequent tribal wars for prisoners to be made slaves by the conquering tribe. Arab traders started the African slave trade by sailing along the African coastline and sending raiding parties to seize people from the tribes living close to the sea. When the Europeans began to exploit Africa's weaknesses there were tribal chiefs who proved only too willing to sell their people for cheap trinkets. If the Spanish and Portuguese were the first major European slaving nations, it was the British who took over and continued the trade.

The slaves were not always passive victims. Sometimes they rebelled against their fate. Significant slave risings occurred in Barbados in 1816, Demerara (Guyana) in 1823 and Jamaica in 1831. These were suppressed with great savagery. This was not simply cruelty for its own sake. It was a sign of how fearful the plantation owners and traders were of an organized slave resistance. They knew that only by maintaining the severest controls could slavery be maintained as a system. Supporters of slavery often argued that slaves lived better lives than they would have done had they been free. The challenge to that is that there is no single recorded case of a freed slave ever choosing to return to servitude.

Attempts to abolish slavery

It is some balm to the liberal mind to know that it was also the British who in the nineteenth century were foremost in attempting to end slavery and the slave trade. Britain formally outlawed the trade on 1807 and abolished slavery in the empire altogether in 1833. British evangelical Christians were prominent in the humanitarian campaigns that led to this. The Royal Navy then used its muscle to impose Britain's new values. It claimed the right to stop and board any ship thought to be a slave carrier; if slaves were discovered the ship was seized. The navy first concentrated on West Africa, where until the trade was broken by the 1860s some 100,000 black slaves were transported annually to the southern USA and Latin America. The navy then turned its attention to East Africa where it harried the Arab traders who each year used the port of Zanzibar to load 30,000 slaves bound for the markets of the Persian Gulf and Arabia.

The crews of Royal Navy ships received a bonus for each slave they freed. There was some attempt to return the released slaves to their original tribal homes, but since the slavers had originally gathered a range of peoples from along the coast, this proved difficult. One compromise solution was to set the freed slaves down in a special area on the Guinea coast, which British abolitionists had established in 1787 as 'the Province of Freedom'. It later became the state of Sierra Leone.

The modern age is baffled and repelled by the readiness with which civilized and informed people in a past age were prepared to tolerate and justify slavery. But it aids historical perspective to remember that the defence they gave rested on a set of basic assertions – slaves were not fully human; they did not really feel pain in its fullest sense; they could not adequately survive on their own – that are essentially the same arguments as are used to justify legal abortion in modern advanced societies.

03 Britain in India and North America

This chapter will cover:
- the South Sea Bubble
- Britain's imperial struggle with France
- Clive and India
- the trial of Warren Hastings
- Pitt and Canada
- the loss of the American colonies.

In the seventeenth century Britain's main enemy overseas had been Spain. In the following century tension with Spain remained, but it was France who became the chief foe. There were two main theatres of Anglo-French rivalry: Canada and India. The Treaty of Utrecht in 1713, which ended the 11-year war of the Spanish Succession with France, had given Britain a number of vital gains for her empire. Among these were the acquisition in North America of Nova Scotia, Newfoundland and the land around Hudson Bay. The growth in her territories was destined to bring Britain into conflict with the French who also wished to extend their own empire in this region. This struggle was to reach a climax in the Seven Years War of 1756–63.

The South Sea Bubble, 1720

Britain's potential for imperial growth after Utrecht produced an astonishing reaction. Between January and September 1720, people in London went mad, mad for money. How little most people understood about finance was startlingly revealed in the fiasco of the South Sea Bubble. Britain came out of the war with France with a national debt of £10 million. An enterprising set of financiers, the South Sea Company, did a deal with the government, offering to take over the debt in return for a repayment interest rate of 6 per cent. The Company was also granted exclusive authority to operate the 'Asiento', the right granted to Britain under the Treaty of Utrecht to monopolize the slave trade between Africa and South America. On the strength of this deal, the South Sea Company offered its stock for public sale. Investors rushed to buy thinking they were on to a very good thing. Encouraged by the take-up, the Company issued even more stock whose price rapidly rose.

Other companies, seeing how eager investors were, offered their stock for sale. Mania set in. Bogus companies set themselves up purely as investment concerns without any real assets. One company invited investment in its programme to discover perpetual motion. Another asked speculators to subscribe two guineas with the promise that it would repay them £200 in two months' time. There was no shortage of takers. None of the speculators understood the basic maxim that what goes up must came down. Even a mathematical genius like Isaac Newton invested in the hope of making a fortune. A total lack of realism prevailed. It could not last. After eight months, South Sea shares had risen to 1,000 per cent of their original price. Realizing how absurdly over inflated these prices were, way beyond any profits they were likely to make as a trading company, the South Sea board decided to sell out before the truth became known. When the news leaked out of what they had done, panic ensued. Prices plummeted, stocks and shares became worthless and people were ruined, including Isaac Newton. The crash taught the investors a bitter lesson. When it comes to money there are always people willing to dupe and be duped.

In the history of Britain's commercial growth the South Sea Bubble was just a blip. Hard-headed traders and gentlemanly capitalists knew that Britain's expanding empire offered them every prospect of real profits. This was especially the case in regard to India.

Clive and India

In 1745 a young man named Robert Clive, the oldest of 13 children, was working as a clerk in the English East India Office in Madras. He was so bored and homesick that he toyed with the idea of suicide. He pointed a gun at himself and pulled the trigger. It jammed. Had the gun's mechanism not been faulty the eighteenth century would have been deprived of an amazing man and an amazing story. Robert Clive was shaken out of his depression by war. In 1746, the army of the French East India Company, seeking to challenge the EEIC's influence in India attacked and seized Madras. With brown dye smeared on his face, and dressed in Indian clothes, Clive escaped through the French lines and made a 100-mile journey to join up with a British force. The Company acknowledged his initiative and courage by immediately awarding him a military commission. If there is such a person as a natural soldier, then Robert Clive was one. William Pitt, the Prime Minister, described him as 'a heaven-born general'. In the five years from 1746 when the French had the larger numbers and held the upper hand, Clive proved brilliant at outmanoeuvring the enemy.

What both the French and British attempted to do was win support from the native princes, among whom there was intense rivalry. Consequently, the military conflicts took the form of joint Anglo-Indian armies facing joint Franco-Indian ones. In the forming of these alliances, intrigue, subversion and double-dealing prevailed. It was a world in which Clive excelled; he delighted in exploiting the antagonisms between the native princes.

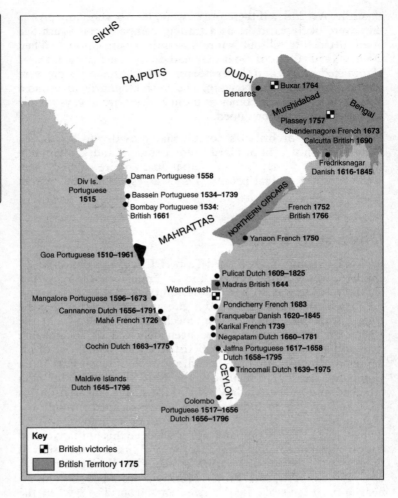

Figure 9 India 1510–1775

Clive's remarkable powers of military command were particularly evident in 1751 when, with a force of only 200 British troops and 300 sepoys (Indian soldiers in the British–Indian army), he successfully defended the town of Arcot against a besieging army of 10,000, made up of French troops and those of the nawab of the Carnatic, who had agreed to co-operate with the French in driving the British out of southern India. The ferocity of Clive's counterassaults eventually broke the siege and the attackers withdrew.

Such was Clive's dominance that by 1754 the French had entirely abandoned their attempt to oust the British from that region of India. Joseph Dupleix, the principal agent of the French East Company, was called home in disgrace. Clive also returned home in 1754, but to a hero's welcome. He responded to his rapturous reception by lavishly spending the prize money that his exploits in India had earned him. But within two years he was back in India. The Company had urgently summoned him to deal with a crisis.

'The black hole of Calcutta', 1756

Siraj-ud-Duala, the Nawab of Bengal, had a deep dislike of the British; he particularly resented the Company's extension of its factory at Fort William in Calcutta which lay within his province. He sent a force to capture the city and seize the Fort. In the aftermath of the attack there occurred an incident which was to become one of the dark legends of British imperial history. Victorian nannies and schoolmasters loved to thrill their charges with the horror of the tale. In the heat of a tropical night, a group of British captives were so tightly crammed into a cell that most them asphyxiated. The precise numbers and the exact size of the cell varied in the telling of the story. One account spoke of 146 prisoners, of whom only 23 survived, in a cell 6 x 6 m (20 x 20 feet) square. Another description had 63 prisoners, 23 survivors, and a cell 4.2 x 5.4 m (14 x 18 feet). Rag-day students at a British university in the 1950s tried to replicate the conditions using the first set of figures; they declared it was physically impossible to fit in so many people, even when they were small and very drunk. But, whatever the exact numbers at Calcutta, there was no disputing a tragedy had taken place. The nawab expressed regret but offered no apology and refused to discipline the perpetrators. He rejected stories that his troops had deliberately mocked the gasping captives all through the night by pouring jugs of water onto the ground outside their cell.

Plassey, 1757

The Company was determined to avenge 'the black hole of Calcutta' and Clive was to be the instrument of vengeance. He sailed from Madras with a small force, recaptured Calcutta, including Fort William, and also found time to batter a French trading post into submission. Clive's suppression of the nawab and his French allies came to a climax in June 1757 at Plassey. It was there that a great pitched battle was fought between Siraj-ud-Duala's 50,000 strong army, supported by French artillery, and Clive's force of 3,000 British and sepoy troops. Luck as well as skill was on Clive's side. A freak storm drenched the nawab's uncovered gunpowder, putting most of his artillery out of action.

Yet Clive knew his force might still be crushed by sheer weight of numbers. He ordered his gunners, who had obeyed the golden rule and kept their powder dry, to fire deliberately at the large targets presented by the bullocks and elephants that carried the nawab's officers and equipment. His aim was not to kill the beasts and bring them down but to injure them so badly that they became crazed and uncontrollable. The gamble paid off; the elephants charged back through their own lines causing havoc. Then, led by Grenadiers of the 39th Foot, the first regular army unit to fight for the East India Company, Clive's force counterattacked, so effectively and successfully, that it suffered only 23 deaths and 49 seriously wounded cases. In contrast, the nawab's army which broke and fled, left thousands of dead behind.

Siraj-ud-Duala was deposed shortly after his defeat and replaced as nawab by Mir Jafar, who, since he owed his position to the Company, was thereafter effectively their man. Jafar also showed his gratitude by handing out large presents. Clive pocketed some £200,000. When criticized for taking so much, he said that since the Company had made over £3 million out of his victories, they should be 'astonished at his own moderation'.

Clive's impact

British gains and French losses in India were formalized in the Treaty of Paris in 1763. The East India Company gained control of Bengal, the richest province in the sub-continent. Appropriately enough, it covered an area the size of France. The French accepted that in future they would not attempt to encroach on established British trading rights in India. Taken together, Clive's triumphs and the Peace of Paris marked a critical stage in the growth of Britain's eastern empire. British military and commercial supremacy in India was recognized and Britain had extended its authority over a further 50 million Indians.

The confidence all this engendered was illustrated by the growth of Madras, Calcutta and Bombay, which, by the end of the eighteenth century, had become centres of international trade. Attracted by what India could now offer ambitious young people – adventure, romance, wealth – many came out from Britain eager to find their fortune or perhaps a husband. An English newspaper sniffily commented: 'Beautiful women are now reckoned among the articles of our export trade to India, not one ship is sailing now without a cargo on board; and they are literally going to market. On their arrival they are shewn as a horse, and are disposed of to the best bidder. This is a coarse description, but does not so indelicate a traffic deserve rebuke?'

Given the glittering prospects India now offered, it was not surprising that corruption, the problem that had bedevilled the East India Company since its foundation, should have intensified. Too many of the EEIC's servants became embezzlers, directing Company profits into their own private funds. It was to put a check on this that the Company turned again to its saviour, Robert Clive. He was asked to do a clean-up job. The task proved as difficult as any of the military challenges he had faced. Between 1765 and 1767 he tried to regularize the taxation system in Bengal which the Company had taken over. To lessen the temptation for employees to fiddle the Company's books or trade fraudulently with its goods, he tried to increase their wages and lower the taxes they paid. The trouble for Clive was that reform is always unpopular with those who see themselves as losing out by it. Moreover, it seemed perverse to them that a man whose dealings in India had made him a nabob should now be denying them the chance to better themselves.

When challenged that he, too, had made money on the side, Clive's answer was yes, he had, but he had worked long hours and years for it. What Clive was against was easy money, or as he put it, 'Rapacity and Luxury; the unreasonable desire of many to acquire [them] in an instant.' You could not just be corrupt, he argued; you had to win the right to be so by achieving something first. The eighteenth-century attitude towards the perks of office is a fascinating one. There was a broad acceptance that perks were a legitimate part of administration, but they had to be earned by long service and they were not to be excessive. It was when those rules were broken that scandal followed. Corruption was not regarded as wrong in itself, since it provided the incentives that made the system run.

Clive had some success in his attempts to streamline the running of the East India Company, but he had made himself a hostage to fortune. When he retired to England in 1772 his enemies closed in on him with accusations that he had been guilty of serious financial malpractice when in India. He was obliged to appear before a parliamentary commission, which in the end, having heard his vigorous self-defence, concluded that while he had taken gifts, any wrongdoing on his part was greatly outweighed by 'his great and meritorious services to his country'. The exoneration was not enough to lift Clive's spirits and he died a depressed man in 1774. There were suggestions that he had taken his own life, but the more likely explanation is that he died of a seizure brought on by the severe stomach disorder from which he had long suffered. He was 50 years old and he had changed the world.

The trial of Warren Hastings

What lay at the heart of the political problems that Clive had faced in his later years was the issue of the nature of Britain's and the Company's relations with India. Was India simply to be a country to be exploited at Britain's whim or did the British have a duty to put Indian interests on a par with their own? This question was highly dramatized in the impeachment of Warren Hastings, the longest trial in English legal history, lasting from 1788 to 1795. Hastings' case was very similar to Clive's. Both men served with distinction in India only to find their methods and their records called into question in England. Hastings had been Governor General of Bengal from 1774 to 1785 in the period that followed Clive's reforms. But whereas the Company had flourished economically in Clive's time, things took a downturn under Hastings. The EEIC's share price dropped from a peak of £280 under Clive in 1768 to a low of £120 at the point Hastings left India in 1785.

It was this that made him enemies. Those who see their profits dwindle are rarely forgiving of those they think responsible. Hastings' reputation was not helped by a terrible famine that struck Bengal in the early 1780s, wiping out five million, one in three of the population; some blamed the severity of the famine on Hastings' taxation policy which had impoverished so many Indians. Led by Edmund Burke, one of the great minds of the day but not a man above vendettas, a group of MPs and peers pressed successfully for Hastings to face impeachment, a special legal proceeding in which parliament acts as a court.

In a trial spread over eight years there were, of course, periods of numbing tedium while lawyers droned on over abstruse points of procedure, but, overall, it was one of the great set pieces of English political and legal history. This was an age of great oratory and during the course of the trial there were many impressive examples of the speaker's art. Burke's opening speech, in which he listed the charges against Hastings, set the standard.

> I impeach him in the name of the English nation, whose ancient honour he has sullied. I impeach him in the name of the people of India, whose rights he has trodden underfoot, and whose country he has turned into a desert. Lastly, in the name of human nature itself, in the name of both sexes, in the name of every age, in the name of every rank, I impeach the common enemy and oppressor of all.

This was great stuff but the substance behind the rhetoric was less impressive. Most of the evidence against Hastings came from the testimony of Sir Philip Francis, a personal rival, who had coveted Hastings' position and power. The two men had fought an indecisive duel.

As to the truth of the charges it is hard to think how, in the circumstances of India in Hastings' time, with constant French interference and fierce rivalry between the princes mixed with frequent changes of allegiance, it was possible to govern effectively without being caught up in intrigue; Hastings had certainly had close dealings with the princes and the Indian people. He had also on occasion been firm with them, perhaps excessively so, but that might be excused as an aspect of strong government. The charge that he became wealthy from his dealings could have been made, as in the case of Clive before him, against any of those who ran the East India Company.

At the trial's end, Hastings was acquitted on all counts, but by then he was a broken man: 'I gave you all and you have rewarded me with confiscation, disgrace and a life of impeachment', he wearily said. Yet, putting the question of his guilt or innocence aside, the impeachment was a watershed in Britain's relations with India. It had helped to establish two key notions; that the British administrators owed as much responsibility to the Indian people as they did to the Company, and that the days of the nabobs when men could look upon India solely as a source for accruing private wealth and privilege were drawing to a close. These changes would not happen overnight but an awareness of responsibility and a recognition of the right of the Indian people ultimately to decide their own fate had dawned.

Such change of attitude had already been hinted at before Warren Hastings' trial had begun. The India Act of 1784 significantly altered the role of the EEIC in India by laying down that the Company was henceforth to share its authority in India with the British government, which would be represented by a Governor General resident in India. What this meant was that although the Company would continue as a commercial concern it would from now on be acting as the ruling agency of the government in Westminster.

Pitt and Canada

At the same time as Clive's exploits in India, equally dramatic events took place in North America where the struggle between Britain and France came to a head. The critical figure in this was the British Prime Minister, William Pitt. As befitted the grandson of the nabob Thomas 'Diamond' Pitt, William was dedicated to the defence of the empire against the French in India and North America. He believed that this could be achieved only through a strong, properly financed and fully-manned navy.

Throughout the Seven Years War of 1756–63, which was fought in Europe, India, and North America, Pitt put his prodigious energies into developing Britain's sea power. The French were never able to match this. If there is one fundamental reason for Britain's eventual success in the conflict, it was France's reluctance to spend enough money on its war effort. This was particularly evident in the French failure to recognize that in a war fought over empire and waged across vast distances, sea power was vital, and therefore, required the maintenance of strong naval forces.

William Pitt, who became the Earl of Chatham in 1766, was described by a contemporary as 'single-minded, imperious, proud, enthusiastic'. He was certainly a man of overwhelming personality. It was said that one frown from him was enough to make people change their mind instantly or certainly swallow what they were going to say. He was not above using his powerful voice to settle an argument he could not otherwise win. He believed literally in standing on ceremony, refusing to allow his staff of secretaries and officials to sit in his presence. He always dressed to impress, wearing a long buttoned coat and full-bottomed wig. Pitt who suffered from gout, a disease associated with excessive consumption of port wine and described by one French doctor as 'the most excruciating pain known to man', always let others know about his agonies. In his office, his crutches and sling were prominently displayed to impress upon official visitors that here was a man who suffered. When an admiral once dared suggest that one of Pitt's war schemes was impossible, Pitt shook his crutches at him and boomed 'Sir, I walk on impossibilities.'

Pitt shared two essential characteristics with two later great war leaders, David Lloyd George and Winston Churchill – a refusal to accept that Britain could be beaten and a capacity to inspire this belief in others. It was said that 'no man entered the Earl's closet, who did not feel himself braver at his return than when he went in'. Yet Pitt, like Churchill, was also a victim of crippling depression. In one episode in 1767–8 he sat for 18 months in a darkened room refusing to come out. It was then that his wife Hester Grenville proved to be his great help-mate by remaining loyal and understanding; without her it is unlikely Pitt could have been guided out of his melancholy.

The struggle for Canada can be told as a tale of two men, the Marquis de Montcalm, the brilliant French commander in North America, and Pitt, who although the civilian Prime Minister, was the great guiding force behind the British effort. What both Montcalm and Pitt realized was that the key to control of Canada was sea power. The tragedy for Montcalm was that he was never able to persuade his French masters of this. The French military made a priority of their land forces, believing that the strength of their various forts in North America would win the day. Montcalm never received the men and supplies that he needed. This enabled Pitt to use the Royal Navy to blockade ports in Europe and North America and so keep the advantage with Britain.

After three years of warfare in three continents success came to Pitt and to Britain in 1759, which became known as 'the year of victories'. The major triumphs were the defeat of the French in the Battle of Minden in Hanover, the capture of French islands in the West Indies and the taking of Quebec in Canada. It was also in 1759 that a large French invasion fleet was smashed by a British naval attack in Quiberon Bay in Brittany before it could set sail for England. All this was celebrated in the song

'Hearts of Oak' whose rousing words and catchy tune made it the chart topper of its day. 'Come, cheer up my lads, 'tis to glory we steer, To add something more to this wonderful year.'

Wolfe and Quebec

The taking of Quebec was as significant for Britain's empire in the west as Clive's success at Plassey had been for her empire in the east. It owed much to Pitt's gift for selecting the best commanders to do his bidding. His choice of James Wolfe to carry out his plans for Canada proved inspired. Like Clive, his great contemporary, Wolfe, was a natural warrior. Although a sickly child, and never fully fit physically as an adult, Wolfe loved war. He devoured books on military theory, going as far back as the Greek writer Herodotus, and then put theory into practice as a rising military star in a series of campaigns in Europe and North America. Wolfe was so possessed and dedicated to his tasks that puns were made about his aggressive sounding name, and it was sometimes rumoured he was mad. When King George II heard this, he said 'Mad, eh? Then I wish he would go and bite some of my other generals.'

Quebec in 1759 proved Wolfe's master stroke. As the map shows, Quebec, which was held by the French under Montcalm, commanded the St Lawrence River, the great waterway into the Great Lakes and French Canada. The British mounted a two-pronged attack. Having seized vital French forts to the south, forces moved up the St Lawrence from the south. Wolfe's troops meanwhile sailed north from Boston, hugged the coast of Nova Scotia and then swung round into the St Lawrence intent on attacking Quebec from the north. Montcalm, however, thought he held two aces. One was time; he calculated that since the British would not arrive until September, they would have to hurry their attack before the winter ice made the river unnavigable to the north. The other was Quebec itself, which was protected by the Heights of Abraham, a range of cliffs which had to be controlled if an effective attack was to be launched. Wolfe's appeal to the navy was 'Put me and my army on the Heights of Abraham, and French America is ours.'

The Navy did just that. Under cover of darkness, and helped by a diversionary bombardment which led the French into thinking the main assault would be at river level, the ships landed Wolfe's troops at the foot of the cliffs from where they tortuously climbed their way to the top. The sailors meanwhile, in an

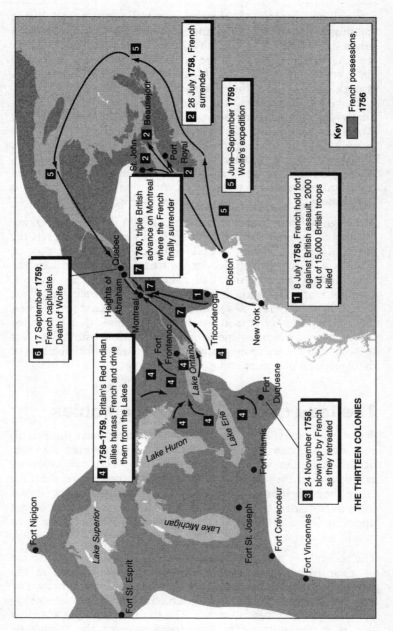

Figure 10 the British conquest of Canada

Key: French possessions, 1756

1 8 July 1758, French hold fort against British assault. 2000 out of 15,000 British troops killed

2 26 July 1758, French surrender

3 24 November 1758, blown up by French as they retreated

4 1758–1759, Britain's Red Indian allies harass French and drive them from the Lakes

5 June–September 1759, Wolfe's expedition

6 17 September 1759, French capitulate. Death of Wolfe

7 1760, triple British advance on Montreal where the French finally surrender

THE THIRTEEN COLONIES

St. John, Port Royal, Beauséjour, Quebec, Heights of Abraham, Montreal, Triconderoga, Boston, New York, Fort Frontenac, Lake Ontario, Lake Erie, Fort Duquesne, Fort Miamis, Lake Huron, Lake Michigan, Fort St. Joseph, Fort Crévecoeur, Fort Vincennes, Lake Superior, Fort Nipigon, Fort St. Esprit astonishing display of physical strength and heavy lifting technique, hauled the guns and ammunition up the cliff face. When dawn came Wolfe was ready to launch his attack. There is a touching legend that in the lull before the assault he re-read his favourite poem, Gray's 'Elegy in a Country Churchyard', remarking 'I would rather have written that than take Quebec.' But take Quebec he did. The fighting was fierce but the French finally capitulated, not, however, before both Montcalm and Wolfe had been killed. There is another story that, as Wolfe lay dying, one of his officers cried, 'Look, Sir they run!' 'Who run?', he asked. 'Sir, the enemy, the French.' With his last breath, Wolfe gasped, 'It is well', and died with a smile on his face. All last words stories have to be taken with a pinch of salt, but it is somehow nice to think he might have said it.

Although fighting continued for a further four years, the taking of Quebec marked the end of French power in Canada. In the Peace of Paris of 1763, France recognized that the whole of Canada was now British. Under the treaty, Britain also kept the West Indian islands she had taken, Grenada, St Vincent, Dominica and Tobago, as well as retaining Senegal in West Africa. With Canada now added to her 13 American colonies, there seemed every reason for Britain to think that she ruled supreme on the North American continent. But within 20 years such thoughts were to be shattered by the successful rebellion of the American colonists.

The loss of the American colonies

By an ironic twist in the imperial story, victory over the French in North America was one of the reasons why within 20 years Britain had lost her American colonies. Why, the colonists asked, should they pay heavy taxes for the upkeep of a British army they no longer needed now that the only major threat from outside had been removed? This led on to an even bigger question. By what right did Britain retain control of the colonies at all?

The reality was that the colonists for over a century had thrived by their own efforts. There was nothing substantial in the economic or political sphere that they needed from Britain, and now that the French threat had been removed there was nothing military that they needed either. The thought also quickly grew that if it was possible to gain freedom from the French by military means, why could the same not be achieved against the

British. The upshot of this was a war against Britain, which produced the Declaration of Independence in July 1776, in which the American colonies asserted their inalienable right to be 'free and independent states'.

The war was a close run thing, a matter of touch and go. The colonists under General George Washington fought with remarkable tenacity and very considerable tactical skill. But if the British generals had had the wit to realize that they were fighting a guerrilla war they might have adapted their strategy more successfully to the conditions. Instead, they stuck too rigidly to marching columns, which left the British troops vulnerable to ambush, and tried to fight in solid square formation only to find that the colonists avoided pitched battles unless it suited them. It was very much a case of a regular army being outwitted and ultimately outfought by irregulars.

After nearly ten years of fighting, the war ended in 1783 with the surrender of the British forces. The ex-colonies proceeded to establish themselves as a new nation, the United States of America (USA), founded on the principles of 'life liberty and the pursuit of happiness'. For a people to take power in this way was a momentous event in imperial and world history.

Various factors explain the American rebellion: the colonists' resentment at being taxed for the benefit of a government 3,000 miles away, their anger at having their trade regulated, their wish to break the laws that prevented them from expanding westward, their desire to worship as they chose, free of the authority of the Anglican church, and their determination to govern themselves in their own parliament. In its simplest terms it was a desire for liberty. The essence of this was captured in 1842 by Levi Preston, a 90-year-old veteran of the War of Independence. When he was asked what had motivated him to fight against the British all those years ago, his eyes flared with long-dimmed fires as he declared: 'What we meant in going for those redcoats was this: we always had governed ourselves, and we always meant to.'

It has been said that in human affairs there is nothing more powerful than an idea whose time had come. The problem is that ideas seldom make headway unless they are backed by force. The American colonists' achievement lay not in the quality of their argument, inspiring though it was, but in their ability to back their demand for freedom with the fire power that obliged the British to accept their terms.

Interestingly, the American War of Independence resulted in the freeing by the colonists of thousands of slaves, an act of gratitude for their fighting against the British. Ironically, however, many more thousands of slaves were freed by the British forces during the course of the war. Canada and the West Indies were the main areas in which the liberated slaves then settled.

Yet the freeing of some slaves at this time amounted to no more than a gesture. The fact remained that the way of life of the southern states of the new nation rested on the institution of slavery. How this state of affairs could be reconciled with the USA's declared principles of freedom and liberty was a question that would take another 80 years before it was finally resolved in a bitter civil war in the 1860s, which saw the victory of the abolitionist north over the slave south.

04

Britain and China

This chapter will cover:
- Britain's first contacts with China
- the clash of cultures
- the opium wars
- the Hong Kong issue.

The McCartney mission

China was an antique land, which, until the late eighteenth century, had been able to preserve its ancient culture by remaining largely detached from other nations. It regarded itself as a unique, self-sufficient society; the name China means 'centre of the earth'. It needed nothing from outside. When foreigners did come to China they tended to be regarded as inferiors by the Chinese, who used terms such as 'barbarians' and 'foreign devils' to describe them. It is true that as early as the sixteenth century Jesuit priests from Portugal and Italy had set up missions in a number of Chinese towns and the port of Macao was later developed by the Portuguese as a trading base. But this was aloof toleration by the Chinese rather than a desire to mix with other people.

When, therefore, in the late eighteenth century Britain made formal requests to the Chinese Emperor, Qianlong, to open his country to British trade the response was lukewarm. Undeterred, the British persisted; they were eager to prevent the Portuguese becoming too influential in Asia. Eventually in 1792 the Emperor said he was prepared to permit a delegation to visit him. Qianlong of the Manchu dynasty ruled China by divine right. Everyone owed allegiance to him; he owed allegiance to no one. To the dignity of his ancient office of emperor that stretched back two millennia, Qianlong could add the venerability that went with age and dynastic experience. At the time of the British visit he was 82 years old, had eight wives, 100 concubines, and had reigned for 57 years.

It was to meet this august, celestial being that in 1792 Lord McCartney sailed in an East India Company ship for far Cathay, the old poetic name for China. His mission was finally received by the Emperor in the autumn of 1793. The proceedings began disastrously. McCartney was an experienced, much travelled diplomat but he was also very British. He did not adjust easily to customs he found degrading. He refused to kowtow to Qianlong. In Chinese tradition kowtowing was obligatory in the Emperor's presence. The practice involved lying face down at full length and tapping the head three times on the ground. This act of prostration had to be repeated twice more so that the forehead touched the floor nine times in all. After that courtiers or visitors were allowed to kneel but they could not look up.

McCartney would have none of this. He saw the kowtow not as an act of respect but of humiliation. The most he was prepared to do was to go down on one knee. Anything further would have been an insult to his God and his King. The Chinese imperial court was appalled. Here was a foreigner, a barbarian from the west, refusing to obey the courtesies that all visitors had to respect when allowed the ultimate privilege of meeting the celestial Emperor. But Lord McCartney, the official representative of King George III, did not see things that way. He was as assured of the superiority of his own culture as the Chinese were of theirs. He frequently referred to Britain in his dispatches as 'the most powerful nation of the globe' and 'the sovereign of the seas'.

Translation added to the incomprehension. The British party had set out with no Chinese speakers. They refused to consider using French priests since they did not trust them to give accurate accounts. Eventually they took along two Chinese priests they picked up in Naples on the way. Unfortunately neither cleric spoke English, so the common language used was Latin. In the discussions with the Emperor, words had to pass from Chinese to Latin to English and back again. This did not prevent communication but it made full understanding difficult. But it did not need words to express the bewilderment and anger of the Chinese at what they saw as a deliberate slight by McCartney. The talks continued but they never fully recovered from McCartney's disregard of Chinese sensitivities.

When the British party left they were given handsome presents of silk and porcelain but the mission had failed. Qianlong let it be known that he had no intention of accepting the British request for trade and a permanent presence in China. He referred to Britain as a vassal state owing allegiance to China. His formal written reply to George III was so dismissive that for a generation British diplomats were prepared to release only a watered-down version of it. The tone of the original can be gathered from an extract from the genuine translation:

> We, by the Grace of Heaven, Emperor, instruct the King of England to take note. We do not have the slightest need of your country's manufacturers. Therefore, O King, we have commanded your tribute envoys to return safely home. You, O King, should simply act in conformity with our wishes by strengthening your loyalty and swearing perpetual obedience so as to ensure that your country may share the blessings of peace.

A French writer later described the McCartney mission as 'a collision of two planets'. It was an apt metaphor, describing how two cultures, each convinced of its own superiority came into conflict. But there could be only one outcome. Despite Qianlong's haughty disdain, China would lose. This was not because of some inherent inferiority. It was simply a matter of technology and fire power. Britain was already an industrial force. Its fighting ships and its weaponry far outmatched anything the Chinese could offer. The British had noted this very clearly during McCartney's visit, one member of the mission remarking, 'I saw not 12 vessels of theirs that could match one of ours.' Once Britain began to use force to back its demand for trade to be opened there was little the Chinese could do to resist. As the nineteenth century wore on, a familiar pattern developed. The British claimed trading rights; the Chinese rejected them; the British sent gunboats to enforce their claims.

Moreover, although the Chinese court was reluctant to admit this, Britain was already trading with China. Tea had been bought from China, where it was called 'cha', as early as the 1670s. Slow to catch on at first, tea, once it had been mixed with milk and sugar, became a hugely popular drink in Britain around the middle of the seventeenth century. Charles II's wife, Catherine of Braganza, did much to make tea drinking fashionable among the upper classes. Every class from landed lords and ladies to factory and farm workers began to drink it as their daily beverage. By 1794 the British were consuming nine million pounds of it a year.

The traffic was not one way. If tea from China had begun to change the habits of the British, the Chinese themselves were being affected in a very profound way by their buying of a particular commodity in return – opium. The difference was that while the British chose to buy tea, the Chinese had little choice about opium. From the 1750s onwards British merchants from India and Burma had established a flourishing but very one-sided trade with China. *Papaver Somniferum*, the opium poppy, is an Indian plant. In 1773 the East India Company claimed a monopoly on the opium trade. The selling of it brought excellent returns for the traders. Indeed, by the 1840s the profits from opium sales to China more than paid for all the tea that Britain bought from China. Calculations also suggest that the opium trade helped pay for Britain's government of India until 1917. But to China it brought both financial loss and social misery: to pay for their imports the Chinese had to use up their silver reserves; more serious still, drug addiction in China's ports and cities began to reach alarming proportions. By 1900 there would be over 14 million Chinese opium addicts.

The Opium Wars, 1839–42, 1856–60

China's pent-up anger at last burst through. In 1839, Emperor Daoguang ordered all British-owned opium to be seized, and forbade further Chinese trade with Britain. When the British merchants protested against this interference, the Foreign Secretary, Lord Palmerston gave them his full support; on his instruction, British warships were sent to China. Gladstone, a future Liberal Prime Minister, condemned Palmerston for pursuing a blatantly immoral policy of forcing opium upon the Chinese people. 'The British flag', said Gladstone, 'is hoisted to protect an infamous contraband traffic.' Palmerston responded by claiming that the Emperor's prohibition was not a matter of morality but an attempt to keep an opium monopoly in the hands of Chinese traders. Palmerston's rallying cry was 'Let us give the Chinese a good thrashing and explain ourselves afterwards.' He gave effect to his words. In the summer of 1840 40 British ships reached the port of Canton which they proceeded to shell. In 1842, after two years ineffective resistance, the Chinese were obliged to sign the Treaty of Nanjing, in which they agreed to renew the opium trade, pay compensation for the opium previously destroyed, and hand over the island of Hong Kong permanently to Britain.

While the Chinese authorities tried to recover as much dignity as they could by coming to terms with Britain, ordinary Chinese were less willing to suppress their anger. Anti-foreigner riots directed against the British and the French, who had quickly moved in to exploit what Britain had begun, became common in the succeeding years. It needed only another incident for war to flare again. This duly arrived in the form of 'the Arrow' affair. In 1856, a Hong Kong vessel, the *Arrow*, sailing under the British flag, was seized by the Chinese after it had been caught flagrantly engaging in piracy and smuggling. The British Consul in Canton demanded both the release of the ship and an apology for the insult to the British flag. When the Chinese authorities were slow to respond, the Governor of Hong Kong ordered the shelling of Canton. As before, the issue divided British opinion. Palmerston, now Prime Minister, took an anti-Chinese stance and backed the owners of the *Arrow* and the British officials. He forced the doubters in his Cabinet into line by asserting that, whatever the merits of the case, Britain's clear duty was to support her representatives in China. He believed the British people were behind him, and showed what a good judge of popular opinion he was by calling, and convincingly winning, a snap election in 1859.

The climax to the war with China came the following year when in retaliation for the murder of French and British negotiators in Beijing, an Anglo-French force attacked the city. In a swathe of destruction, the troops razed or burned some of Beijing's most ancient and most beautiful buildings, including the famed imperial Summer Palace. The French novelist, Victor Hugo lamented bitterly:

> Once, in a distant corner of the world, there was a great wonder, a wonder known as the Summer Palace. This wonder is no more. There came a day when two bandits entered that Palace. One plundered it, the other put it to the torch. We Europeans are civilized, and to us the Chinese are barbarians. Here is what civilization has done to barbarism. History shall call one of these bandits France, the other England.

The eventual outcome was that in 1860 the Chinese were forced to sign another humiliating peace treaty, the Beijing Convention, in which it accepted Britain's demands and gave over Kowloon harbour to the British.

Attention is now naturally focused on British abuses, but the Opium Wars, unacceptable as they are to a later generation, were at the time a relatively small sideshow. China was much more concerned with an internal revolt. The Taiping Rebellion, a peasant revolt which occupied the years 1850–64 and cost the lives of some 30 million Chinese during the course of its suppression by the Emperor's armies.

Britain's humbling of China was the cue for other European powers to impose themselves. In a series of 'unequal treaties' signed over the next half century, China opened some 50 'treaty ports' to foreign powers, most notably France and Germany. The ports were key strategic or commercial sites, dotted along China's coastline and rivers. In addition, a number of Chinese cities witnessed the creation of 'concession' areas; these were defined parts of cities and ports within which European law and customs held sway. The Chinese were treated as strangers in their own land. The concessions functioned as a series of foreign mini-states within China's borders.

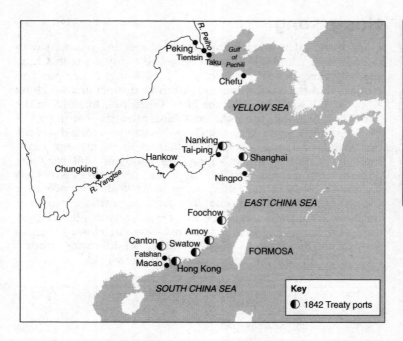

Figure 11 China 1839–1900, showing treaty ports and concession areas

In many ways the grab for concessions was an extension to Asia of the European scramble for Africa (see Chapter 08). However, China was not colonized in the same way as Africa. With some exceptions, such as the British in Hong Kong and the Portuguese in Macao, the Europeans did not directly govern China, which formally remained a sovereign state. The pattern adopted by the European powers was to establish their own enclaves within China. When the Chinese tried to resist they were invariably suppressed. This was glaringly revealed in the Boxer Rising of 1898–1901 when an 11-power international army that included British forces crushed a desperate attempt by a Chinese nationalist movement, led by the Qing royal house, to drive out 'the foreign devils'.

Hong Kong

Hong Kong offers a fascinating study of Britain's relations with the Chinese. Although Britain controlled many areas in China she only ever owned one colony – Hong Kong. A key point to stress is that the colony consisted of three distinct areas – Hong Kong island, Kowloon, and the New Territories. In 1842, in the Treaty of Nanjing, imposed on China after its defeat by the British in the Opium War, the Qing dynasty was forced to cede the island of Hong Kong to Britain on a permanent basis. Eighteen years later in the Beijing Convention of 1860 the Qing government granted Britain, again in perpetuity, Kowloon harbour directly facing Hong Kong. In 1898 Britain took over the rest of Kowloon peninsula. This fresh acquisition, known as the New Territories, was not ceded permanently this time but on a 99-year lease. The British Crown Colony of Hong Kong, so formed in 1898, was to develop during the following century into one of the most prosperous cities in the world.

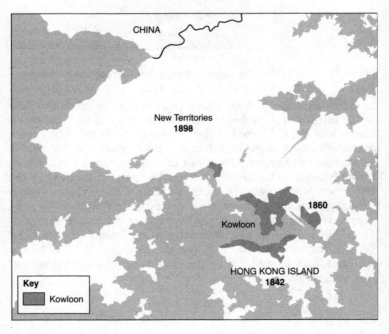

Figure 12 Hong Kong

It was in the second half of the twentieth century that this phenomenal growth occurred. By this time, Hong Kong was Britain's only remaining possession in China. This was because during the war against Japan, Britain, as a gesture of goodwill towards her Chinese ally, had renounced all her other claims to territory and authority in China. It was after the Second World War that Hong Kong took off as a commercial force. Its position as a British outpost within China gave it an obvious attraction to those fleeing from the Communist takeover of the Chinese mainland, which was completed in 1949 with the creation under Mao Zedong of the People's Republic of China (PRC).

Hong Kong now became a haven for thousands of businessmen and bankers who brought their wealth with them. Many came from Shanghai, hitherto the richest area of China. They became the entrepreneurs of Hong Kong, developing new lines of manufacturing based on shrewd estimates of the needs and tastes of a growing world market and achieved at low cost by the unscrupulous use of cheap refugee labour. In the 1970s a booming tourist industry added to the colony's expanding wealth. Despite a brief recession in the mid-1980s, Hong Kong continued its economic growth. Such was the demand for land in an increasingly overcrowded area that a property boom occurred in the eighties, helping to create a new class of super-rich financiers.

Problems between China and Britain over Hong Kong

Hong Kong's economic miracle was both a reproach and an inspiration to China's Communist rulers. The city's capitalist success contrasted sharply with the low growth rate of socialist China. Yet at the same time it offered the prospect of the PRC's acquiring this dynamic commercial city 'the pearl of the Orient' in 1997 when Britain's lease expired.

But would Britain ultimately be willing to hand over its colony to what it regarded as a repressive regime? What the Chinese government feared was that the British would insist on retaining Hong Kong island in accordance with their entitlement under the original Nanjing Treaty. To Beijing's surprise, it was Britain which made the opening move when Margaret Thatcher, the first British Prime Minister to visit China while in office, went to Beijing intent on resolving the issue. It is arguable that her eagerness to reach a settlement played into Beijing's hands, since it helped the PRC, which had previously been unsure about what diplomatic line to adopt, to begin the negotiations from a position of strength. Britain's formal approach enabled the Chinese to make the matter of sovereignty the central issue. The PRC, led by Deng Xiaoping, an experienced and wily negotiator, adopted an uncompromising stance; it would settle for nothing less than the complete return of Hong Kong to China. There was no question of Britain's leasehold being extended; 'I would rather see Hong Kong torched than leave Britain to rule it after 1997', Deng told Mrs Thatcher.

The strength of Deng's feelings convinced Thatcher that sovereignty was not negotiable. She realized that Britain would have to attempt to make the best of a bad job by obtaining concessions on less central matters. The option of giving up the New Territories but retaining Hong Kong island and Kowloon, which technically Britain was entitled to do under the original agreements, was never seriously considered. Logistically, there was no possibility of the colony's surviving separately once China had recovered the Kowloon peninsula. The New Territories were much larger in area than Hong Kong, and it was through them that the essential water and power supplies flowed to the island. Simple geography would make it impossible for the British to keep Hong Kong supplied from outside. In one irate outburst Deng told Thatcher that 'the Chinese could walk in and take Hong Kong later today if they wanted to.'

Deng may have been play-acting a little, but there was real anger behind his words. It was his view that the treaties they were now discussing as if they had solemn binding weight had been originally wrung from a weak Chinese government by Britain's naked, aggressive imperialism. Hong Kong had been a violent seizure by Britain. As China's official newspaper, *The People's Daily*, now put it: 'One hundred and fifty years ago, to maintain its drug trafficking in China, Britain launched the aggressive Opium War against China, during which it carried out burning, killing, rape, and plunder on Chinese soil.'

The Joint Declaration, 1984

Sharp though the exchanges between Deng Xiaoping and Margaret Thatcher were, they did help to open the way for an eventual compromise. In the Sino-British Joint Declaration of

December 1984, Britain agreed that when the lease on the New Territories expired in 1997 sovereignty over the whole Hong Kong area would revert to the PRC. On their side the Chinese Communists made a commitment to leave the economic structure of the territory substantially unaltered; Hong Kong would remain a capitalist 'Special Administrative Region' (SAR) until 2047.

The agreements reached gave promise of a smooth transition towards Chinese rule of Hong Kong. However, in June 1989 everything was thrown into doubt by the news of the Tiananmen Square massacre when the Chinese government sent in the army to disperse a pro-democracy demonstration. The obvious question arose: if the PRC could shoot down its own people in its own capital of what value were the promises it had given regarding Hong Kong? From that moment on relations between Britain and Communist China grew increasingly strained as the time for the 1997 handover approached.

Matters became sharply personalized with the appointment in 1992 of Christopher Patten as the last British Governor of Hong Kong. Patten made it his aim to create a 'through train, that is to establish as much democracy as possible in Hong Kong before Britain's departure so that the incoming Communist administration would find representative institutions already in place'. Beijing reacted furiously. Its bitterness was understandable. Britain was only a belated convert to democracy in Hong Kong. During its previous 150 year administration she had made no attempt to introduce representative government into the colony. All public positions had been filled by British appointees, not elected spokesmen of the Hong Kong people.

Yet although Patten was vilified in the Chinese press as a 'fat liar' he was also criticized by Hong Kong's democrats who felt increasingly let down by what they regarded as Britain's surrender to Beijing. Even after Tiananmen Square had revealed how ruthless the PRC could be, China continued to be accorded all the niceties of diplomatic protocol as if there were no question of Britain distrusting the regime. Critics accused the Foreign Office of playing a 'charade of deplorable dishonesty' to cover up the fact that Britain was selling the Hong Kong people short. The 'selling' could be taken literally, it was suggested. By this was meant that from the beginning of the negotiations Britain's aim had been to avoid upsetting the PRC so as not to jeopardize the great economic returns that her potential trade with China's one billion people would bring.

In the end, Britain simply decided to trust the Chinese to do what they had promised. Edward Heath, a former British Prime Minister and an honoured guest in the PRC, even argued that the different histories of China and the West made it inappropriate to judge the two cultures by the same political standards. He suggested that it was unrealistic to expect Beijing to apply Western forms of democracy in Hong Kong or any other of its territories. Heath's was precisely the type of reasoning that offended the island's democratic parties who argued that it exemplified Britain's attempt to keep its conscience clear while surrendering the Hong Kong people to a repressive regime.

Developments since the 1997 handover have not provided a wholly clear answer as to how oppressive that regime would prove to be. Believers in China's good faith remain confident; doubters are not convinced.

05

the Pacific and Australasia

This chapter will cover:
- Cook's Pacific voyages
- the founding of Australia and New Zealand.

James Cook

'Gentlemen, next year 1769, will be a great year for the astronomers amongst us. 1769 will see the passing of the planet Venus across the face of the sun.' These words by the President of the Royal Society set in chain a series of events that were to have momentous consequences for Britain's empire. What excited astronomers was the opportunity provided by the eclipse to measure the earth's distance from the sun. But, to do this accurately, the measurements had to be taken from different latitudes. One of the key vantage points chosen was the island of Tahiti in the south Pacific. Initially the Royal Society and the Admiralty fought over who should lead the expedition. The Society wanted a prominent scientist; the Admiralty wanted a great sailor. Eventually the Admiralty won; it was their man, James Cook, who was appointed. In selecting him, they had chosen arguably the ablest seaman and navigator in maritime history.

Born in 1728, Cook was a Whitby lad, one of eight children in a poor farm labouring family. At the age of 12 he began to learn his mariner's skills aboard the collier ships that carried coal from Whitby either across the North Sea to Holland or along the coast to the port of London. Cook always said that the finest ships were the Whitby colliers; later, when he had the freedom to choose, he insisted that it was these that carry him on his voyages. In 1755, at the age of 27, he joined the Royal Navy. He showed extraordinary talent as a map maker. In 1759, it was his accurate charting of the St Lawrence River, carried out while being shelled by the French, that enabled British forces to take Quebec (see page 48). He stayed in the Canada station for a number of years, mapping the rivers and eastern coastline.

Cook's voyages

It was his understanding of applied mathematics, particularly trigonometry, that earned Cook his reputation and brought him to the attention of the scientific world and the Admiralty. Lieutenant Cook left London in the *Endeavour*, carrying 70 crew men and 12 scientists in August 1768, and reached Tahiti after a seven-month journey in March 1769. He stayed there for three months, observing the passage of Venus across the sun in June and making important measurements and calculations. But that was only part of the story. His commission from the Admiralty also required him to search for '*Terra Australis*

Incognita', 'the Unknown Southern Continent', south of Tahiti. There was still a general belief up to the time of Cook's voyages that in the southern hemisphere there was a huge land mass that began between the Indian and Pacific Oceans and stretched down to the Antarctic. It was thought that in the 1660s the Dutch explorer, Abel Tasman, had discovered the eastern part of this mass in the area that he had called Van Dieman's land. Obeying Admiralty instructions, Cook proceeded to sail the *Endeavour* as far south as latitude 40°. He did not find the great southern continent but what he did discover were the separate lands of Australia and New Zealand, whose eastern coasts he carefully charted. He also put in at various points on the Australian shore, including an area which he christened Botany Bay in honour of the botanists on board. Cook then headed for home.

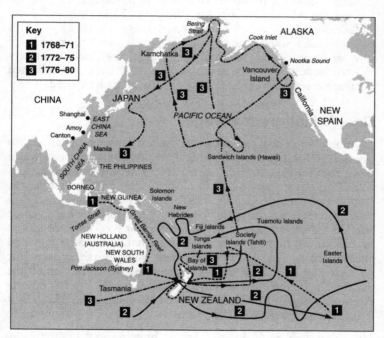

Figure 13 Cook's main voyages

It proved a hazardous journey. At one point, the *Endeavour* ran aground on the Great Barrier Reef, the coral shelf off Australia's north-east coast. Large gashes appeared in the hull, but the crew managed to float her off and at the same time make running repairs. Cook continued calmly to chart the reef and its waters. Ferocious storms threatened to capsize the ship as it made its way through the straits dividing the northern tip of Australia and New Guinea. Fuller repairs were possible when the ship, its crew laid low by malaria and dysentery, limped into Batavia on the island of Java. The *Endeavour* eventually arrived back in England in July 1771, after a round journey of three years.

Within a year Cook was back at sea leading another expedition in two new Whitby-built colliers, *Resolution* and *Adventure*. They were fitting names for Cook and his enterprise. His aim was again to find the great southern continent. In a wide sweeping arc he sailed south into the Antarctic circle, the first known mariner to have done so, swung north to land in New Zealand, then on to the Pacific islands of Tonga, Fiji, Easter Island, the Marquesas Islands, the New Hebrides, and New Caledonia. It was an amazing voyage even by Cook's extraordinary standards. As well as conclusively proving there was no continuous southern continent, he had accurately charted huge areas of the south and central Pacific and collected invaluable botanical specimens from the lands he visited.

Cook's last great voyage

In June 1776, Cook embarked on the third, and what proved to be the last, of his great commissioned voyages. His objective was a quest that had fascinated and frustrated explorers for centuries – the finding of a north-east or a north-west passage linking the Pacific and Atlantic Oceans. Cook first travelled south to Tahiti where he revisited the native peoples with whom he had formed friendships eight years earlier at the time of the Venusian eclipse and to whom he now gave gifts of animals, including pigs and sheep, sent by George III. Cook then sailed north, crossed the equator and laid claim to a set of islands, which he named the Sandwich Islands after Lord Sandwich, the head of the Admiralty. One of the islands which he visited was Hawaii; it was later to prove fateful for Cook.

His ships then made for the Arctic, hugging and mapping the western coast of North America. It is interesting to reflect that at the very time Cook was doing this, the American colonists in the east of the continent were engaged in a war for their independence from Britain. Cook's efforts to find the longed-for passage came to nothing. Pack ice and ice flows prevented his making any progress. Disappointed, he turned back and sailed

for the Sandwich Islands, putting in at Hawaii for repairs and
fresh supplies.

His reception on arrival there staggered him. He was treated as
a god. At first he did not understand that his return to the island
seemed to fulfil a local prophesy that foretold that a Polynesian
god would return to the island. Gifts were showered on Cook
and his party. Laden with these, the *Resolution* and *Adventure*
attempted to sail away. However, the *Resolution*'s rigging was
damaged in a gale after only two days out and the ship had to
return to the island. This time the reception was far less
welcoming. The visitors' previous stay had angered the islanders
who resented being told by their chiefs they had to give so much
to them. Violence flared when Cook, claiming that the islanders
had stolen a ship's boat, tried to take one of the chiefs hostage
until it was returned. The chief's warrior bodyguard fought
back. Cook was knocked down and hacked to death.

No matter how tragic his end, James Cook had added hugely to
human knowledge. In a little less than a decade he had explored
and charted vast areas of the Pacific from the Arctic to the
Antarctic. He had contributed enormously to science – to
medicine, biology, botany, zoology, geography, meteorology,
anthropology, oceanography – and to the empire.

Cook's significance

There were two especially remarkable features of Cook's later
voyages that demand to be noted. One was his trial of a time
piece specially designed for use at sea by the English
watchmaker, John Harrison. Such was the watch's balance and
strength, that it kept perfect time despite the rolling of the ship.
It was this device that revolutionized navigation by making it
possible to plot longitude with complete accuracy since precise
time fixes could now be made.

The other notable feature was the carrying of limes on board.
Scurvy was a highly unpleasant disease that particularly affected
sailors who spent long periods at sea. Common symptoms were
painful joints, dizziness, a persistent feeling of tiredness, and
painful mouth ulcers which swelled and bled and eventually
caused the teeth to fall out. The condition was a result of
vitamin deficiency. Lime juice, which is rich in vitamin C proved
a highly successful cure. Having discovered this, Cook
demanded that limes be a basic part of his ships' provisions. So
effective was this practice that by the end of the eighteenth

century lime juice was being regularly given by the British navy to its crews. The term 'limey' came into the language around this time to describe British sailors and is still sometimes used by teasing Americans in reference to the British generally. There is a persistent myth that in the days of sailing scurvy was the great killer disease at sea, but while it certainly caused great suffering, it was not scurvy but dysentery that claimed the largest number of crewmen's lives.

The use of lime juice was an aspect of Cook's very progressive approach to health and hygiene. He demanded that, when circumstances allowed it, his crews should wash in fresh water. He also required that the ships' decks be regularly scrubbed and the quarters be kept as clean as possible. These were tedious chores which the sailors muttered about, but the beneficial results were undeniable. Very few of his crews died from disease during the voyages he led.

Australia

One almost immediate consequence of Cook's exploration of the east Australian coast was that Britain chose to use the area as a dumping ground for its unwanted. On 26 January 1788, after a nine-month voyage, six ships carrying 737 male and female convicts, guarded by 200 marines, landed in a harbour which was given the name Sydney, after the Colonial Secretary of the day. The original site had been Botany Bay, but Captain Arthur Phillip in charge of the convict fleet and soon to be the first Governor of New South Wales as the south-east region was called, found Sydney a much easier bay for landing. Over the next 80 years before transportation was finally ended in 1868, some 162,00 convicts were sent to Australia. Few would have believed when the prison colony was first created that Australia was destined to become a great dominion and a great modern nation.

The convicts, about a quarter of whom were Irish, were a mixed bunch. Some were hardened criminals whom it would not be nice to know, some were persistent thieves, and some were unlucky victims of a legal system that, overwhelmed by the rapid increase in petty crime that accompanied the growth of population in London and Britain's industrial areas in the eighteenth century, turned to transportation as a means of avoiding the problem. As a judge in one of the London courts put it: 'I sentence you to what I do not know, perhaps to storm and shipwreck, perhaps to infectious disorder, perhaps to famine, to be massacred by savages, perhaps to be devoured by wild beasts.'

In time, as Australia showed that it was possible to build a stable and potentially prosperous society from the apparently unpromising human material with which it had all begun, the new land came to attract free colonists. Only a dribble came at first because of the length of the journey and the relatively high cost and discomfort of the passage. But then incentives overtook fears. The quality, extent and cheap price of grazing and farm land of the interior (initially only 5 shillings an acre) brought the shepherds, farmers and stockmen. By 1817 the first settlements began in the territory of Victoria where Melbourne became a major centre. Settlers began to develop areas of Western Australia in 1826. By 1836 South Australia had been founded with Adelaide as its key port of entry. These developments owed much to the initiative of Edward Gibbon Wakefield who believed that emigration from Britain to the colonies should be put on an organized basis. He took to heart the population theories of Thomas Malthus and believed that the growing number of people in Britain would soon outstrip food supply. The only way to avoid a disaster, Wakefield argued, was to thin Britain's population by spreading it around the colonies. Wakefield was a colourful character; he wrote a long study of land reform in Australia while serving a three-year prison sentence in England for running off with an under-age heiress.

A major stimulus to emigration came with the discovery of gold in the 1850s first in New South Wales and then in Victoria, whose population leapt from 70,000 in 1850 to 333,000 five years later. In the decade after 1850, the population of Australia overall grew from 400,000 to 1 million. Forty years later in 1901, such had been its progress, that it formally became the Commonwealth of Australia, made up of New South Wales, Queensland, Victoria, South Australia, Tasmania, and Western Australia. Long before that it had already attained independent dominion status.

A problem which was never satisfactorily resolved in the first century and more of its existence was white Australia's relations with the indigenous nomadic people of the continent. The Aborigines, whose culture was traceable back some 40,000 years, were a hunter-gatherer people. Their apparent backwardness made them despised figures in the eyes of most of the early European settlers. The tragedy that followed from this is powerfully illustrated in the adventures of one young man who came to settle in Australia.

Jorgen Jorgensen – an Australian settler

In 1794 a 14-year-old lad named Jorgen Jorgensen, who lived in Copenhagen, was looking for adventure. Spotting that a British coal-carrier tied up in the harbour did not keep a tight check on who came aboard, he stowed away under some sacking. So began a lifelong love affair with the sea and with Britain. By the time he had reached his twenties he had become first mate on the *Lady Nelson* mapping the coast of what became New South Wales. Australia was to play a major part in his extraordinary life. In 1804 he helped found a settlement at Hobart on the island of Van Diemen's Land (Tasmania). Having returned to England by way of Tahiti he fought against his native Denmark in the English victory in the Battle of Copenhagen in 1807. Jorgensen then turned his attention to Iceland; so successful was he in exploring and mapping the area that he acquired the mock title of 'King of Iceland'.

Despite his elevation to royalty, back in England he got into trouble gambling, which led to his being imprisoned more than once for debt. After a failed attempt between 1815 and 1817 to make his fortune in Europe, he returned to London where again he fell foul of the law. He was convicted of stealing linen from the house where he was boarding and sentenced to be transported. However, he did a deal with the court in which he promised to make his own way to Australia, thereby saving the cost of conveying him there. However, when he was found still living in London a year later, he was arrested as an escaped convict, a charge that carried the death penalty. His popularity saved him; a flood of petitions led to the sentence being commuted to the original transportation.

As a result he found himself once more in Tasmania, but this time as a prisoner. Nothing daunted, he used his skill and experience to make himself indispensable to the colonial administrators. Jorgensen was given the responsibility for establishing relations with the native Aborigines. His task was not to come to friendly terms with them – they were hated by the colonists as killers and thieves for their raids on the white settlements – but to help organize the 'Black Line', a plan in which the whites would combine to drive the Aborigines off the island altogether. The 'Black Line' was the idea of Governor Arthur who thought in uncompromising terms of kill or be killed; if they did not destroy the Aborigines, the Aborigines would destroy them. In what is difficult to describe as other than an act of genocide, the native Tasmanians, who were a separate race from the mainland Aborigines, were ruthlessly suppressed to the point of extinction, the last of them dying in 1876.

It was the saddest of tragedies. James Cook had earlier spoken glowingly of the aboriginal way of life as being in many ways happier than that of the Europeans. Yet many colonists believed that the disappearance of the Aborigine was inevitable; he could not expect to survive in the new Australia. It was not dissimilar from the view of the American colonists towards the native Americans whose culture they destroyed. All that can be said in mitigation is that extermination was never official British government policy in Australia. Indeed, in 1838 there was an attempt to prevent the exploitation or abuse of the native peoples. Yet despite such good intentions, the European impact on the native Australians was a disruptive one, particularly in regard to health. The strains of disease which the Europeans brought with them decimated the Aborigines who had no natural resistance to such virus-based conditions as influenza. In the course of the nineteenth century their number dropped from around a quarter of a million to a mere 50,000.

Mary Reibey – an Australian settler

Today on the Australian 20-dollar note, there is a woman's picture. It is of Mary Reibey, who died in Sydney in 1855. Her story provides a remarkable insight into the working of the empire and the peopling of Australia. Born Mary Haydock in Bury, Lancashire, in 1777, she was one of a large working-class family. Her parents died when she was ten and she was left to fend for herself. Her natural high spirits made her good company but also led her into trouble. When she had just turned 13 she was charged with stealing a horse. What made her suspect in the eyes of the court was that at the time of the alleged theft she was wearing boy's clothes. She was found guilty and sentenced to seven years' transportation. After a grim voyage in which her bright manner made her a favourite among her fellow prisoners, she eventually arrived in Sydney in 1792. She wrote a letter back to an aunt in Blackburn in which she promised to make the best of her situation. She was to prove true to her word in a way not even she could have known.

Her first position was as an unpaid domestic servant in a family home. Then in 1794 at the age of 17 she married Thomas Reibey, an Irishman she had met on the voyage. She bore him seven children in 12 years. Reibey was an entrepreneur. He had been an employee of the East India Company and put his experience and contacts to good use to develop a large import–export company in Australia. He became a major landowner in Sydney. However, since his business meant he was away for long periods, Mary became increasingly involved in the running of the company. On her husband's death in 1811, Mary, now aged 34, inherited his business and his property.

She chose to continue running the company rather than sell it off. She inherited several farms and a fleet of ships that traded with the Pacific Islands, China and India. Under her management the business flourished and by 1820 she had amassed a fortune of £20,000. She went back to England intending to fade into comfortable retirement. But Australia was now in her blood. She said she missed the openness both of its scenery and its people. Within a year she had returned to Australia, this time with no intention of leaving.

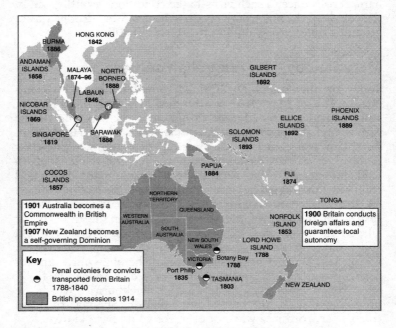

Figure 14 British expansion in the South East, 1788–1914

She continued to help run the company, but branched out into charity work. Over the last 30 years of her life she became known and respected as a formidable but kind old lady, eventually dying in 1855 at the age of 88. She was truly one of the first great female pioneers of the empire.

New Zealand

A similar difficulty to Australia's in the relations between natives and settlers occurred in the development of New Zealand. White contact with this region had begun in the early nineteenth century but it hardly had an auspicious start. The first settlers to arrive were escaped convicts from New South Wales and dubious traders intent on selling contraband whisky to the native people, the Maoris. In 1809 a few Christian missionaries arrived, who did their best to prevent the abuse of the natives. It was not that the Maoris were pushovers; far from it. They were tough people with a fierce warrior tradition. It was rather that, unused to the European financial and trading methods, they were often cheated. Gibbon Wakefield was prominent in the next move. He helped create the New Zealand Association which was responsible for 1,200 colonists settling in the country in 1839.

The British government then responded to pressure to impose order on New Zealand by annexing it in 1840, empowering the Governor of New South Wales to run the country. The Treaty of Waitangi was agreed between Britain and the Maori chiefs in the same year. Under this, the Maoris accepted Britain's sovereignty in return for recognition of their land ownership and rights. But, as the Maoris saw it, Britain did not keep her side of the bargain. White settlers encroached on Maori lands in disregard of the Treaty while the British authorities did nothing to prevent it. The New Zealand Association cynically dismissed the Treaty as 'a praiseworthy device for amusing and pacifying the savages for the moment'.

The Maoris' sense of betrayal led to the inevitable outcome. A series of wars between Maori warriors and British forces blighted the years 1845–72; the Maoris lost 2,000 in the struggle, the British 560. The wars did not stop the flow of immigration, which was quickened by the discovery in 1852 of gold in South Island; by the 1870s white settlers outnumbered the indigenous people by a quarter of a million to 50,000. It was this demographic shift that ultimately condemned the Maoris to defeat. They had to make the compromise of preserving what they could of their separate culture by acknowledging that the white settlers were the dominant force in New Zealand. They accepted membership of the New Zealand Assembly as a token political recompense for what they had lost culturally.

06 the grand imperialists

This chapter will cover:
- Raffles and Singapore
- Brooke and Borneo
- Palmerston's gunboat diplomacy
- Disraeli's expansive imperialism.

Three remarkable men illustrate Britain's approach to empire. In their different ways they showed how individual the imperial impulse was. The chosen three tell us much about Britain's relations with the Far East and Africa.

Stamford Raffles

The Raffles Hotel still stands in Singapore. It does not quite have the atmosphere it once did. But the décor remains splendid and the imaginative tourist can still visualize what it must have been like in the high days of empire. It is a fitting monument to one of the great imperialists of the early nineteenth century – Sir Stamford Raffles.

In February 1805, Olivia Fancourt, a recently widowed lady, called at the offices of the East India Company in Penang, to enquire about her pension rights. A young assistant administrator, who had just taken up his post, was asked to deal with her. Their eyes met and it was love at first sight. Within a month they were married. The young man was Stamford Raffles, aged 25, nine years younger than his wife. He was to be a key figure in the expansion of the British empire in the east. When Raffles arrived there, Penang, an island in the Malacca Straits off the Malay peninsula, a region rich in spices, rubber and oil, had just been taken over by Britain after pushing out the Dutch and the French. Malaya was also very rich in its mixture of peoples and faiths. Indians, Chinese and Arabs had settled there to work and trade, bringing with them their Hindu, Islamic and Buddhist beliefs. Raffles was very open to experience. He was stimulated by his new surroundings; a keen botanist and a zoologist, he was fascinated by the peoples of the area and by its flora and fauna.

His energies and attractive personality, allied to his administrative skills, saw him make a rapid rise. Everyone who met him immediately liked him. Within two years of his coming to Penang he had been appointed Chief Secretary to the British Governor General in Malaya. It was while he was holding this post that he became convinced that Britain needed to consolidate its influence in the region by taking the island of Java. That it was currently held by the Dutch he regarded as a minor problem. It was largely in response to Raffles's urging that a British naval force seized Java in 1811. He was immediately made Governor. Raffles endeared himself to the Javanese; he made a point of going among them to listen to their problems and offer solutions. He also found time to study and record the local wildlife.

But his love affair with Java was short lived. In the territorial rearrangements made under the Treaty of Versailles at the end of the Napoleonic wars in 1815, Java was given back to the Dutch. His sense of personal loss, intensified by the death of his beloved Olivia, seemed as if it might destroy Raffles, who was already a sick man. He had been weakened also by suggestions that he had misappropriated funds. There was no truth to the charge, which was made by an embittered military commander, General Gillespie. The downside of Raffles's popularity was that it also created jealousy in people of lesser talent.

Waved off by adoring thousands, Raffles left Java in 1816 and arrived in England the following year to find that news of his achievements had preceded him. The East India Company agreed to an official enquiry which cleared his name. He was knighted and his scientific work, which included a published study of Java, was recognized by his being elected to the Royal Society. These successes renewed his spirits and his energy and he eagerly accepted the offer of the governorship of Bencoolen in Sumatra.

Singapore

Bencoolen was not the most prominent of places but it was enough to re-stimulate Raffles's quest for empire. In 1819, using his charm and negotiating gifts, he cut through a host of legal difficulties to persuade the Sultan of Johore to lease to Britain at a nominal rent the island of Singapore on the southern tip of the Malay peninsula. It proved a master stroke. At the time Singapore was 200 square miles of mangrove swamp. Only a few hundred people lived there, mainly fishermen and pirates, who used it as a hideaway. But Raffles saw its potential. 'This place possesses an excellent harbour, it is within a week's sailing of China, close to Siam and at the very seat of Malaya – in fact Singapore is everything we could desire.' His judgement proved impeccable. Over the next century and a half the island he had had the foresight to take over for Britain became one of the world's major ports and an international centre of trade and finance. It also provided Britain with a vital naval base which, until its capture by the Japanese in 1942, allowed the Royal Navy to rule the waves east of Suez.

Raffles lived to see none of this. The ill-health that had continually dogged him forced him to retire to England in 1823, after less than a year as the first Governor of Singapore. He still had the energy to be an active founder member of both the Zoological Society and the London Zoo before dying at the age of 45 in 1826.

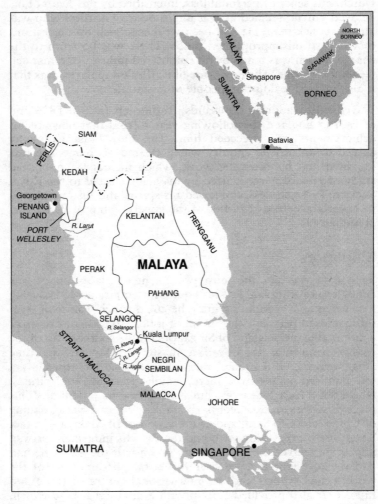

Figure 15 the world of Raffles and Brooke

Brooke and Borneo

Raffles's inspiration outlived him. Empire building at this stage was very much a matter of individualism and initiative. Great deeds were achieved, lands were claimed, and the British government then recognized what had been done. James Brooke followed the path that Raffles had so successfully laid down. Born in India in 1803, Brooke was excited from a young age by the thought of adventure. At 16, he became a soldier in the East India Company for which his father worked. Like Raffles, Brooke believed that the Indonesian islands offered the greatest chance for British expansion. He set his sights on Sarawak, a northern province of Borneo. In 1838, financing himself with the money left him by his father, he chartered ships, raised an army and set sail.

Again, like his hero Raffles, Brooke was an adept negotiator. Knowing that Sarawak, which was under the overall authority of the Sultan of Brunei, was disputed between various tribes, Brooke went directly to the Sultan and asked to be allowed to create a permanent British base and settlement in the region. In return, he promised the Sultan that he would impose order on the troublesome area and also protect the Sultan's ships from the pirates who plagued the South China Seas. Somewhat hesitantly, the Sultan granted his wish. Brooke duly made a number of sorties against rebel tribes, playing them off against each other and gaining victory as much by threat and bluff as by direct attack. But where he was sincere was in his wish to improve the lot of the local people, many of whom for generations had suffered repression from corrupt rulers. His reforming policies in Sarawak, once he had achieved a measure of control, endeared him to the people. The Sultan of Brunei now became an enthusiastic supporter of Brooke and the British. The climax to this extraordinary imperial escapade came in November 1841, when Brooke, in a grand ceremony which he helped to devise, was installed as Governor and Rajah of Sarawak.

Not only did Brooke extend the empire in the east, he founded a dynasty. Both his son and grandson son succeeded him to the throne of Sarawak. His line became known as the 'White Rajahs'.

Lord Palmerston

If any one statesman could be regarded as epitomizing British imperialism at its most confident and its most domineering, a strong contender would be Henry Temple, Viscount Palmerston, who served as either Foreign Secretary or Prime Minister for 26 of the 35 years between 1830 and 1865.

The Don Pacifico Affair, 1850

In Athens one evening in 1847 a bunch of drunken rowdies started a riot. To keep up the fun they decided to take it out on the Jews who lived along the Piraeus, the port area of the Greek capital. One of their victims was Don Pacifico, a Jewish trader from Portugal, who happened to be living in Athens. He was roughed up, some of his goods were thrown into the harbour, and his house was set alight. A small incident in world terms, it was soon magnified into a matter of international law and Britain's good name.

Pacifico claimed compensation from the Greeks and appealed to the British authorities to support him. His case was that, since he had been born in the British colony of Gibraltar, he had a right to British citizenship and, therefore, to British protection. Pacifico had long been notorious as a shady character and he greatly overvalued his losses. He claimed, for example, that the fire at his house had destroyed £26,000 worth of irreplaceable documents, though he declined to say what these were. Palmerston, as Foreign Secretary, chose to ignore the rumours about Pacifico's reputation, and took up the cudgels on his behalf. Learning that the Greek authorities were unwilling to consider Pacifico's claims for damages, Palmerston, without consulting his Cabinet colleagues, ordered British gunboats to be sent to Athens to seize Greek ships. When the matter was debated in the House of Commons in 1850, he came under fire from some quarters for his 'reckless diplomacy'. Palmerston fought back in typical style. His concluding words to the speech in which he justified his actions captured the public imagination and made him hugely popular in the country at large.

> As the Roman, in days of old, held himself free from indignity when he could say, 'Civis Romanus sum' [I am a Roman citizen], so also a British subject, in whatever land he may be, shall feel confident that the watchful eye and the strong arm of England will protect him against injustice and wrong.

Palmerston and the Queen

Overblown rhetoric this may have been, but it was what ordinary people wanted to hear. Palmerston had already acquired a reputation for putting foreigners in their place and for ignoring the courtesies and protocol attaching to his office. He once remarked that one Englishman was worth ten Russians. Queen Victoria and Prince Albert were frequently left seething by his simply not bothering to keep them informed about foreign affairs. In 1850 Palmerston caused a diplomatic furore when he backed a group of London brewery workers after they had assaulted General Haynau, an Austrian general, who was making an official visit to Britain. Mindful of the way Haynau two years earlier had brutally crushed popular anti-Austrian risings in Italy and Hungary by hanging men and flogging women, the draymen first jeered at 'General Hyena' and then physically attacked him. He was rescued but not before his clothes had been torn and his voluminous whiskers pulled.

On learning of the incident, Palmerston remarked it was a pity the workers had not 'tossed him in a blanket, rolled him in the kennel, and then sent him home in a cab'. A furious Victoria demanded that her Foreign Secretary formally apologize to the Austrian government for such remarks. Palmerston did indeed write a formal letter but only to complain to the Austrians that they should not have sent a brute like Haynau to England in the first place. When it was discovered that Palmerston had not shown his letter to the Queen before sending it, the royal court was outraged while in popular taverns the news of his latest exploits was raucously cheered.

Palmerston's style of imperialism

Palmerston was once described as a liberal abroad and a conservative at home. It was certainly the case that he often gave strong support to liberal anti-government movements in other countries. This may have been as much a wish simply to rile and embarrass foreign governments as to promote progressive causes, but it helped suggest that in its imperial might Britain also had rights. This could lead to a remarkable inversion of values. Nowhere was this more evident than in his relations with China, as described in Chapter 04.

It was Palmerston's character as much as his policies that put the gloss on his brand of imperialism. His bluff style, his enthusiasm, his abiding cheerfulness, physical vigour and deep patriotism characterized him throughout his long life. Until his late seventies, he rowed or swum daily before breakfast, then went horse riding after. Only months before his death at the age of 81, he sat down to a meal consisting of: two bowls of turtle soup, pâté, cod with oyster sauce, and a dish of mutton and ham. He then started on the main course – pheasant.

Yet for all Palmerston's commitment to British interests, he was not looking for ways of extending British settlement abroad. Despite his patriotism and striking ability to catch the public mood, his policy was essentially to respond to problems as they arose, not to follow a consistent effort to expand overseas. That form of imperialism is more accurately associated with the great Conservative leader Benjamin Disraeli.

Benjamin Disraeli

In many personal respects, Disraeli matched Palmerston. Both were 'characters' with a feel for what would now be called public relations. As a young man Disraeli deliberately dressed outrageously in order to make himself known. He once turned up at a public function dressed in a green velvet suit with a yellow waistcoat. Like Palmerston, he could turn on the charm, especially with the ladies. But there was a difference in regard to one particular lady – the Queen herself. Whereas Palmerston had irritated Victoria, Disraeli flattered, beguiled, and delighted her. Their relationship had the air of a genteel flirtation. He was the only one of her prime ministers she allowed to sit down in her presence. There was calculation in Disraeli's charming manner. He saw the monarchy as the centre around which to build a new notion of empire. It was during his time that British politics became increasingly democratic. Many more people gained the vote, so it became important for political parties to be able to appeal on a broad front. Disraeli judged that imperialism would be a vote winner with the growing electorate. It proved a shrewd move. Far more people in Britain favoured expansion overseas than opposed it.

From the early 1870s, Disraeli began to express a clear commitment to the empire as an essential aspect of Conservatism. He was encouraged in this by the attitude of his great political rival, the Liberal leader, William Gladstone, who was hostile to any form of foreign involvement. Disraeli publicized his own party's attitude towards empire in a series of powerful campaigns in the early 1870s. It was part of his programme to convince the voters that Gladstone's Liberal governments were destroying the nation's true character. Denouncing the Liberal attempts to reduce Britain's status as an overseas and imperial power, Disraeli pledged his party to the restoration and enlargement of the empire. The way Disraeli put his imperialist ideas into practice can be see in four characteristic episodes.

The purchase of the Suez Canal shares, 1875

In 1875, the bankrupt ruler of Egypt, the Khedive, was forced to sell off his holdings in the Suez Canal project, that was currently being constructed under French direction. Disraeli jumped in to seize the opportunity. He used his influence with Rothschilds, the European banking giants, to raise the necessary capital to purchase the shares for Britain. He wrote exultantly to the Queen: 'You have it, Madam; the French Government has been outgeneralled. The entire interest of the Khedive is now yours.' Disraeli announced in Parliament that the route to India was now secured. He was hardly exaggerating. Britain was now effectively in control of the world's most important man-made waterway, linking East and West. She had also extended her influence into the eastern Mediterranean and North Africa and made Egypt an area of special British concern. This was to have far-reaching consequences.

Not everyone was as pleased as the Queen by Disraeli's move. His old adversary, Gladstone gave a striking expression of the anti-imperialist argument of the day.

What is the meaning of safeguarding the road to India? It seems to mean this; that a little island at the end of the world, having possession of an enormous territory at the other end of the world, is entitled to say with respect to every land and every sea lying between its shores and any part of that enormous possession, that it has a preferential right to the possession or control of that intermediate territory. That is a monstrous claim.

(*W. E. Gladstone in the Commons, Dec. 1876*)

The Queen as Empress of India, 1876

The following year Disraeli introduced the Royal Titles Bill, which conferred on the Queen the title of 'Empress of India', thus making her the personification of the imperial idea. He calculated that people in Britain and the colonies would have a much stronger and clearer sense of the meaning of empire if they could relate it to a particular person. Victoria, enchanted by what Disraeli had done, sent him a Christmas card, signed 'Regina et Imperatrix' [Queen and Empress].

The Afghan War, 1879–81

Disraeli's determination to resist any challenge to Britain's position in India, 'the jewel in the Crown', led directly to a crisis over Afghanistan, India's north-western neighbour. Worried by Russia's expansion into southern Asia, which by the 1870s appeared to threaten India, Disraeli felt it necessary for Britain to take control of Afghanistan as a buffer state. When Sher Ali, the Afghan Amir, resisted Britain's demands that he reject Russian overtures and accept British authority, an army was dispatched from India to compel him to comply. This brought on the Afghan War of 1879–81, which proved a British success militarily but one which offended Liberal opinion and led to renewed denunciations of Disraeli's disregard of morality in state affairs. Gladstone was subsequently to reverse Britain's aggressive policy in the region.

The Zulu War, 1879

In 1876, Disraeli dispatched a British army to the Transvaal in support of the Dutch Boers in their war with the native Zulus. His intention was not primarily to aid the Boers but to assert British authority in southern Africa. Things went badly at first. The Zulus, under their great leader, Lobengula, inflicted a major defeat on the British forces at Isandhlwana in 1879 before being finally overcome later that same year at Ulundi.

Disraeli died in 1881, just too soon to see the great explosion in British expansion in Africa that his enthusiastic imperialism had done so much to promote.

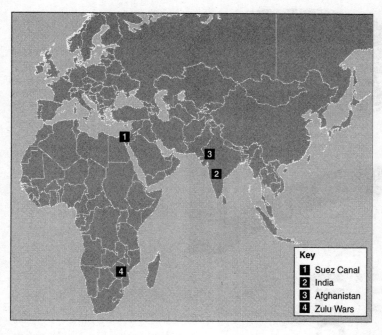

Figure 16 key areas associated with Disraeli's imperialism

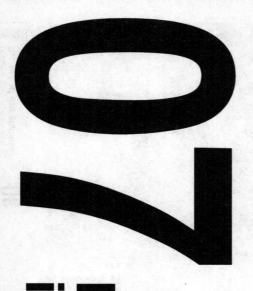

07

India – the jewel in the Crown

This chapter will cover:
- the clash of cultures in India
- the Indian mutiny
- the Great Game
- the life of the Indian princes
- the Curzon era.

The loss of the American colonies had the effect of concentrating Britain's thoughts on her eastern empire of which India was the centrepiece, the 'jewel in the Crown'. Yet this was not a formally-adopted policy directed from Westminster. Individual enterprise and initiative were still the driving force behind imperial expansion.

The clash of cultures – Thuggee

The three men, Kasim, Miraj, and Narbada, were friendly and well behaved. When they asked the party of five travellers whether they could join them so as to increase their mutual protection while journeying on the lawless roads, they were made welcome. Over the next two days they became the life and soul of the party, entertaining their new-found friends with songs and stories. Then on the third night, one of the group was woken by Kasim and Miraj and asked excitedly to come outside to see something remarkable. When they reached the courtyard, Kasim and Miraj said, 'Look, look, up into the sky.' As the traveller raised his head, Narbada stepped from the shadows swiftly slipped a cord around his neck and garrotted him. The three then stripped the body of its clothes and valuables, slit it open and buried it. Over the next hour the other four travellers were murdered in the same way.

Kasim, Miraj and Narbada belonged to the Thuggee sect, a religious cult whose members believed it was their sacred duty in the service of the goddess Kali to commit ritual murder. In 1826, Colonel William Sleeman, the district officer for Jubbulpore in north-east India, who had a genuine concern and affection for the Indian people, decided to put a stop to the murderous practice, which was reckoned to have taken the lives of some 50,000 travellers since the British had been in India. He pieced together what he knew of the cult, learning that it ran in families with fathers initiating their sons into the sacred rites. He came to understand that it depended on anonymity – members invariably committed their murders outside their own local areas – and on the fact that ordinary Indians were too scared of reprisals to give evidence against the sect.

Sleeman decided on a policy of exposure. He ordered mass arrests of suspects, partly so that systematic interrogations could be conducted and partly to show the people that the thuggees were not beyond the reach of law and punishment and, therefore, could be testified against and denounced. The policy worked. When the arrested Thugs realized the game was up, they seemed proud to boast of their fearsome record. One sect member admitted to over 1,000 killings, adding 'there were many more, but I ceased counting when sure of my thousand'. He may well have been exaggerating out of bravado, but his sense of self-justification could not have been clearer.

Fittingly enough, 504 of those arrested were hanged for their admitted crimes. Sleeman built steadily on his success and in 1835 made his campaign a nationwide affair. By 1848 some 4,500 Thugs had been rounded up. This marked the end of the practice of murder, if not of the cult itself. Eventually everyone, Indians and British alike, came to rejoice in the destruction of thuggee. Even those most critical of Britain's interfering with Indian customs accepted that the saving of innocent lives from the predations of brutal killers far outweighed any supposed slight to local traditions. Revisionist historians have suggested from time to time that the British magnified the Thug menace in order to justify their hold on India, but there seems little doubt that the threat was real enough, whatever its true scale, and that its extinction was an unmixed blessing for the people of India.

Suttee

There was less unanimity in the reaction to another campaign in India – the attack upon suttee. This was a tradition which required that a widow submit to being burned alive with her husband's body on the funeral pyre. Although this practice had some basis in Hindu religious belief in reincarnation, the principal reason for its continuation was that the death of the wife cleared the way for the inheritance to go to the next generation. Sons did not try too hard to dissuade their mother from showing her loyalty to their dear departed father by immolating herself. The thought of the money coming their way made them able to bear their double grief with fortitude. The complications of inheritance were also the reason for the female infanticide that occurred in some parts of India. The ritual sacrifice of young girls was justified on the grounds that it left a larger pot of money for the male heirs of the family.

Lord William Bentinck, Governor General from 1828 to 1835 and a strong evangelical in religion, ran a campaign similar to William Sleeman's. Measures were introduced under him to outlaw suttee. He had some success, but he met difficulties.

Unlike thuggee, which few could defend as other than plain murder, suttee belonged to a genuine social tradition, however repellent it might appear to Western eyes. How far Western sensibilities should be allowed to interfere with local tradition was a conundrum that was never fully resolved throughout the history of the empire. Bentinck also had the problem that the authority of the Raj was never absolute in India. Despite a series of wars in the 1830s and 1840s which saw the defeat of the Afghans and the Sikhs and the annexation of Sind, Oudh, the Punjab and parts of Burma, the fact remained that the princes held sway in their own territories and what went on there was outside British jurisdiction. At the funeral in the Punjab in 1839 of Prince Ranjit Singh, four widows and seven concubines were burned alive on his pyre. When three of the women rushed screaming from the fire they were pushed back into the flames by men wielding long poles.

Indian grievances

An important measure was passed in the British parliament during Bentinck's time as Governor General. A particularly significant sentence in the India Act of 1833 declared that 'the interests of the native subjects are to be consulted in preference to those of the Europeans whenever the two come into conflict.' This may have been the intention but it did not always work that way. The fact was that those British who came to India, often with their families, as administrators, soldiers, engineers, missionaries and medical staff – came to be an exclusive governing and privileged class who seldom mixed with the local peoples except in the relationship of master and servant.

Greased cartridges

In the Indian army, the standard technique in preparing a bullet for firing was for the rifleman to bite off the greased paper casing around it to release the gunpowder. It was this technique that in 1857 produced a mutiny, the largest challenge to British rule in India there had ever been. The Dum Dum munitions factory in Calcutta had produced a new type of cartridge for use in the latest model of the Enfield rifle. It was the fats used to grease the cartridge that caused the trouble. Rumours quickly spread that these were a mixture of pig lard and beef fat. When the Muslim sepoys were told how the cartridges they had been issued were greased they hurled their ammunition pouches to the ground and spat violently to clear their mouths of contamination. Lard was an abomination to Muslims since it came from pigs, regarded as unclean beasts. The Hindu sepoys did not spit but recoiled in horror. Beef fat was unacceptable to them, not from abhorrence but from a sense of sacrilege. In Hindu practice it was forbidden to eat the flesh of the cow, a sacred animal.

Had the dispute merely been about greased cartridges, it would have soon been over, since their issue was stopped immediately after the first complaint was voiced. Mutton fat was substituted. But in truth the question of the animal fats was only a pretext for the rising. What underlay it all was the issue that in a sense had been simmering ever since Britain first took hold of India – for how long would the Indian peoples accept their subordination to the British. Even when the British administrators, missionaries and soldiers acted in good faith and with goodwill towards the Indian people, and this was not always the case, there was no escaping the basic fact that the Indian people were governed by foreigners.

In that sense what caused the Indian mutiny was the problem which dogged Britain's relations with all its imperial possessions throughout the history of the empire. The administrators, priests, nuns, doctors and nurses invariably came with the intention of doing good. But that was the root of the trouble. The notion of doing good derived from a sense of superiority. The Europeans considered they had something to offer that the native peoples could not produce or develop if left to themselves. It was this that often alienated colonized peoples. In India, for example, the introduction of western-style schools and hospitals were unalloyed benefits in British eyes. But the cultural cost was often too high for the Indians. Education, medicine and surgery were usually associated with religious missions. The very visible presence of the teaching and nursing orders of priests, brothers and nuns was a cultural affront to many Indians.

The shock of the new

On 16 April 1853, the first train in India carried 400 passengers the 20 miles from Bombay to Thana. (Within 50 years railways were to spread across the whole of the country and provide work for more Indians than any other activity.) India was coming into a new age, as the telegraph poles that had begun to dot the skyline also testified. Such developments could inspire wonder but they could also bring alienation. How quickly life was changing can be measured by the time it took for a message to reach Calcutta from London:

- 1770 – seven months, by coach, sailing ship, and runner
- 1840 – four weeks, by coach, steam ship, and runner
- 1854 – less than one day, by telegraph.

An important enterprise was undertaken in the Great Trigonometrical Survey, which, between 1802 and 1880, mapped nearly the whole of India. This included the precise measurement of the world's tallest mountain, named after the survey's leader, George Everest. Since foreigners were not allowed to travel in Tibet or Nepal, the surveyors dressed themselves in the robes of Buddhist monks. One of the party, Nain Singh, spent many years in Tibet walking in what seemed to be an oddly exaggerated way that amused or bemused the local people. He was in fact taking steps of exactly the same length, using prayer beads and a compass concealed in a prayer wheel to record his paces.

The rumour about the cartridges came on top of a list of grievances that had been building up among the sepoys, the Indian troops. Here the religious and caste differences proved critical. The sepoys recruited from Bengal were mainly Hindu, many of them high caste. Over the generations they had come to regard their army service as a mark of their distinction and justifiable privilege. They resented having to serve alongside lower castes in the ranks. This was an especially touchy matter when it came to service overseas since this meant the soldiers were likely to have to travel in crowded troopships. New regiments recruited in the provinces that Britain annexed in the early nineteenth century added to the problem. Ghurkhas from Nepal, Sikhs from Kashmir and Muslims from the Punjab were now part of the British army. It was a volatile mix.

Other developments added to Indian anger. Imported goods had been allowed to flood in, ruining local producers and traders. The behaviour of some English wives did not help. Around this time, a larger proportion than was usual in British armies overseas had joined their husbands. They pushed Indian mistresses aside and acted in a haughty and superior manner towards the sepoys. In themselves these things would not have caused mutiny but they helped to create an atmosphere of resentment out of which more serious troubles grew.

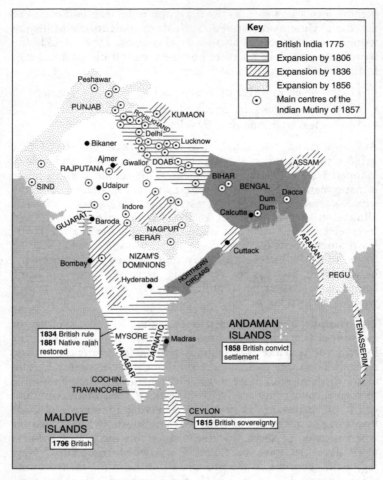

Figure 17 the british in India by 1857

The Indian mutiny, 1857–8

The Mutiny began at Meerut when the sepoys refused to handle the cartridges. When an attempt was made to imprison all those involved, the troops rose up and killed their British officers. They then marched to Delhi where they obliged the Mogul Emperor, the 82-year-old Bahadur Shah, to declare himself their leader. But it was no more than a gesture. He was too old and too reluctant to be anything more than a symbol. Although there were pockets of anti-British resistance right across northern India, the key centres of the rebellion were Delhi, Lucknow and Cawnpore. It took four months for the British to retake Delhi, and over a year to recover Lucknow and Cawnpore. It was not surprising that some of the fiercest resistance took place in the last two places named. They were both in Oudh, a province annexed by the British only a year earlier. The struggle there was what would now be called a war of national liberation.

The fighting was often brutal and savage on both sides. Extraordinary courage was also displayed by civilians as well as troops. Among the European women taken prisoner during the rebel siege of Cawnpore was Harriet Tytler, a soldier's wife. She had her infant daughter with her. Unable to stop the child from fretting and crying, Harriet found a terrifying way of pacifying her. She took a knife and sliced her own feet so that they bled freely; she then encouraged the toddler to play the game of being nurse. In Harriet's own words: 'No sooner did my wounds heal, than she used to make them bleed again for the simple pleasure of stopping the blood with my handkerchief. But it had the desired effect of amusing her for hours.'

Although it was a mutiny, the majority of troops stayed loyal to their British commandeers. The Indian princes also backed the British. This is what made it in some ways a civil war as much as an anti-British struggle. Had the Indians been united, it is hard to think the British could have overcome them. Sheer numbers would have decided the matter. At the time of the mutiny, of the quarter of a million soldiers who formed the Indian army barely 40,000 were white.

British reactions to the mutiny

In Britain the mutiny was presented in over-simplified terms. Little attempt was made to explain the subtleties of the question or to explore the Indian grievances that underlay it. It was described as a rebellion against lawful authority, which therefore justified the most severe reprisals. And severe these certainly were. They make disturbing reading to a modern audience. Before their hanging, the mutineers defeated at Cawnpore were made to lick the encrusted blood off the bodies of those they had killed. In a letter that appeared in *The Times*, a British soldier described how a group of prisoners were tied across the barrel of a field gun and blown to pieces:

Some of the 200 prisoners have been tried, and we blew 40 of them away from our guns in the presence of the whole force; a fearful but necessary example, which has struck terror into their souls. Such a scene I hope never again to witness – human trunks, heads, legs, arms, etc., flying about in all directions. I trust and believe we have done what duty demands.

Far from being appalled by such retribution, many in England found it a fitting response. It was a leading preacher of the day who declared to loud applause from his congregation: 'The religion of the Hindoos is no more than a mass of the rankest filth. The Gods they worship are not entitled to the least atom of respect.'

Yet when passions had cooled there were those in India and Britain who were prepared to act upon the lesson the mutiny had taught them. There was a growing recognition in Britain that reforms were needed. A Government of India Act in 1858 disbanded the East India Company, transferred administration to a new India Department, appointed a Viceroy and established a Legislative Council. Now, for the first time, Britain directly ruled India.

The great game

The jolt that the Mutiny had given Britain strengthened her determination to keep India as the centrepiece of the empire. A consistent element in Britain's foreign policy was its concern to protect India and the routes to it. This is what explains the suspicion shown by all British governments towards Russia. It was fear of Russian expansion that had motivated much of the foreign policy before 1914. This was often summarized as 'the great game', referring to Britain's alertness to the Russian threat to India. A whole series of wars, now largely forgotten, were fought by Britain as a check on Russia. The taking of Afghanistan, Tibet and provinces of northern India itself were all intended to create barriers to Russian expansion. The region known as the North-West frontier, where Russia and India meet, became a favourite setting for the novels, poems and dramas of the Victorian and Edwardian eras. Boys in Britain thrilled to the tales of derring-do in the Hindu Kush, the Khyber Pass, and the Himalayas.

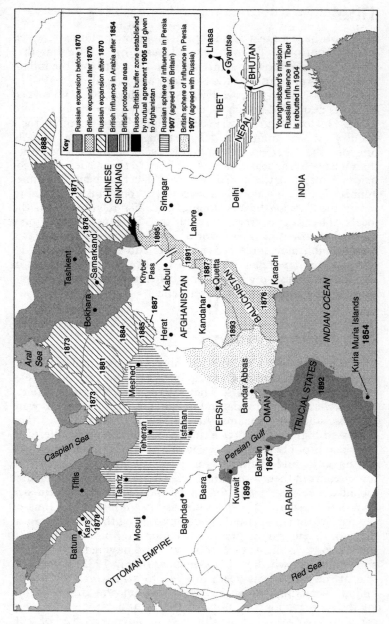

Figure 18 the area of the Great Game

Tibet

In one of the last great acts in the great game, Britain attempted to take control of Tibet. It was all based on a false fear that Russia was about to move into the area. Lord Curzon, the Indian viceroy, was anxious that the Russians be forestalled. In 1903, a 40-year-old English colonel, Francis Younghusband, who owned 67 shirts and loved taking ice-cold baths, led an expedition into Tibet. He found no Russians there but the presence in their country of his uninvited 1,200-strong British army finally offended the Tibetans, who initially had been indifferent rather than hostile to the expedition. A number of skirmishes occurred, before a major battle ended with 900 Tibetans being machine-gunned. It was all tragically unnecessary. Younghusband tried to repair the damage by developing friendlier relations with the locals. The British troops taught the Tibetans how to play football on the roof of the world. The eventual outcome was a treaty establishing trade between Tibet and India, which in the end did not amount to very much since the government in London, anxious now to develop better relations with Russia, chose not to implement the agreement.

The Indian princes

Another result of the mutiny was an even closer understanding between Britain and the Indian princes. The princes were a remarkable set of leaders. They carried various titles. Hindu princes were usually rajahs and maharajas, Muslim princes were nawabs, sultans or nizams. At the height of their power they possessed extraordinary wealth. An outstanding example were the Nizams of Hyderabad, a province of central India renowned for its gold and diamond mines. This line of princes had inherited from their forebears a collection of precious items that included priceless jade, the rarest porcelain, and giant-size diamonds. Osman Ali, who ruled as Nizam during the time of the two world wars, could lay claim to being the richest man in the world. He was a great benefactor of Britain giving £20 million towards the war effort in 1914 and buying fighter planes and equipment worth twice as much as that in 1939. It was said that at the time of his death in 1946 he was worth over £500 billion. Something of an eccentric, Ali ate and drank hardly anything, surviving on nuts, cigarettes and opium. His only ostentatious display of wealth was in buying a fleet of 200 luxury cars.

Lord Curzon

If there is one individual who may be said to have typified the British imperial administrator it was Curzon. While still a student at Oxford he wrote a verse that left no doubt about his self-belief:

My name is George Nathaniel Curzon
I am a most superior person.
My hair is soft, my face is sleek
I dine at Blenheim twice a week.

Yet despite his undoubted wit, style and ability, he lived in physical pain all his life, a fact unknown to all but his closest associates. A twisted spine meant he had to wear a special corset. It held him upright and added to his haughty air. But his disability did not prevent his becoming a prodigious traveller. Among the places he had visited by the time he was 40 were the USA, Russia, Japan, China, Afghanistan, Singapore, Ceylon and Siam. His great love was Asia, in particular India, whose possession, he believed was the main source of Britain's imperial pride and strength.

Curzon, having held various posts in the Indian and Foreign Offices between 1891 and 1898, had made himself popular by resigning from the government in protest against its sluggish defence of British imperial interests when threatened by German advances in China and French aggression in Siam. As a reward, or perhaps to shut him up, Salisbury, the Prime Minister, made Curzon a lord and appointed him Viceroy of India. Curzon loved it. The regalia, the ceremony, and the splendour appealed hugely to him. In a sense he became the greatest of the Indian princes. The outstanding example of this was the Delhi Durbar held in 1903. Officially, this great gathering was held to honour the coronation of Edward VII, but Curzon turned the occasion into a magnificent display of power of the princes and of Britain. Vast processions of courts and peoples, officials and armies, horses and elephants, drawn from across the whole sub-continent, took days to pass by the throne and pay homage to Curzon, sitting as Edward's representative. In the words of a typical account, it was:

a magnificent sight, and all descriptions must fail to give an adequate idea of its character, its brilliancy of colour and its ever-changing features, the variety of howdahs and trappings and the gorgeousness of the dress adorning the persons of the Chiefs who followed in the wake of the Viceroy.

But Curzon was not simply a superb imperial showman. Behind the pageantry there was a firm political purpose. His aim was to prove that British and Indian interests coincided. That was why he buttered up the princes who, at the start of the twentieth century, ruled nearly a third of India. What he wanted was a form of princely rule of India with Britain acting the role of the major prince. But it was a policy that was, arguably, already out of date when the twentieth century began. Rather than winning the princes over, the manner in which he treated them as prefects with himself as the head boy, left them disgruntled.

Curzon also upset the other two thirds of India. He declined to promote Indians to top positions in the administrative system and explained his reluctance by declaring, 'The highly placed native is apt to be unequal to the task.' The result was that he alienated the very class of Indians whom Britain had sought to win over after the mutiny by inviting them to build their careers in the civil service. These young educated professionals felt they had been betrayed; rather than co-operating with Britain, they now became supporters of Indian independence.

Not all Curzon's policies were failures; he helped to create better relations with Afghanistan and so safeguard India's North-West frontier, did much to promote educational standards, and travelled energetically around India attempting to resolve land disputes. But when he proposed the partition of Bengal he offended Hindu and Muslim interests. He was recalled home in 1905.

He stayed in politics for another 20 years until his death in 1924, playing a major role in many of the key domestic and foreign issues of the day. He remained a larger than life character, his home becoming a centre of social gossip and political intrigue. There was talk of his becoming leader of the Conservative Party, but he never quite made it. An inner party report referred to him as representing the type of privileged politics that 'no longer has a place in this democratic age'. It was a comment that might equally be applied to him as viceroy in India. There was something essentially dated about his attitude and style. He belonged to an era of India's history that was passing. The India of the twentieth century would belong to the Indians.

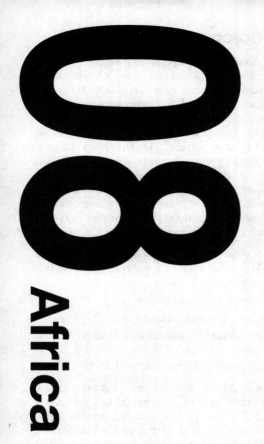

08

Africa

This chapter will cover:
- the European scramble for Africa
- Britain's part in this
- problems in Egypt and the Sudan
- the Anglo-Boer war
- the growth of African national consciousness.

The European colonization of Africa

Around 1870 a critical phase in modern history began with the 'scramble for Africa'. This was a movement in which the major European powers competed with each other to claim territories overseas which they then developed as expressions of their national strength, pride and ambition. The competition was spread across the world but the outstanding example of European imperial rivalry was Africa. As the map shows, between 1870 and 1914 the European powers – France, Britain, Germany, Spain, Portugal, and Belgium – engaged in a massive land grab. In 1870, the interior of Africa, known to the early Victorians as the 'dark continent' was still largely unexplored. By 1914 the whole vast continent had been partitioned between the major European powers.

Britain took an enormous share of the spoils. In the half century before the First World War, she acquired or consolidated her hold over the following regions of Africa:

- **north Africa** – Egypt and the Sudan
- **west Africa** – Gambia, Sierra Leone, Gold Coast, Nigeria
- **central and southern Africa** – Rhodesia, South Africa, Bechuanaland, Nyasaland
- **east Africa** – Uganda, Zanzibar, Kenya, Somaliland.

Despite its eventual gains in Africa, Britain came into the race a little late. It is one of the many ironies of imperial history that it was Disraeli's great rival Gladstone, the anti-imperialist, who entered Britain into the race, though that was not his intention. Gladstone had condemned Disraeli for his imperial polices that were 'deliberately designed to stifle liberty'. Yet it was Gladstone who began Britain's scramble for Africa by occupying Egypt in 1882.

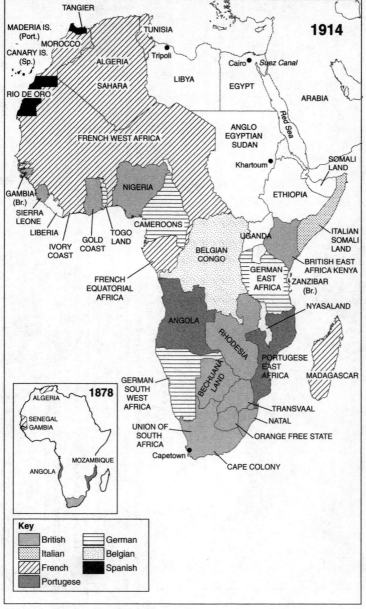

Figure 19 the scramble for Africa, 1870–1914

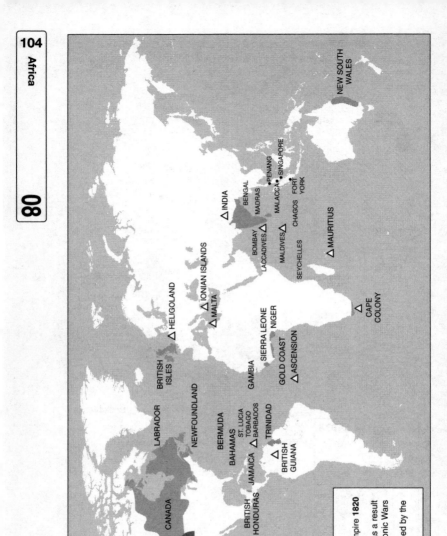

Figure 20 the British empire in 1820

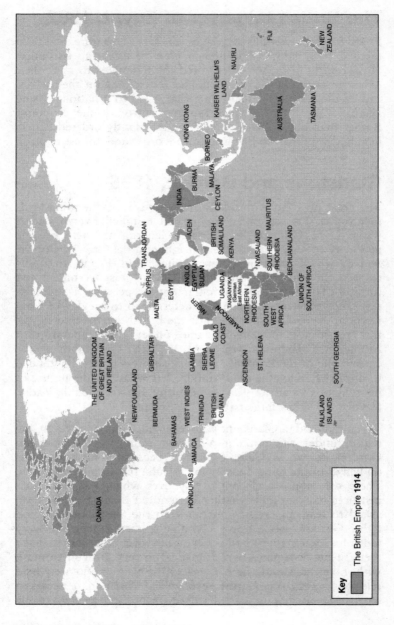

Figure 21 the British empire in 1914

The British takeover of Egypt, 1882

In 1878 a bankrupt Egypt, part of the Turkish Empire, had been rescued by a joint Anglo-French plan of financial assistance. However, the plan, which required the Egyptians to meet their debts by imposing severe economic restrictions on themselves, caused the people such suffering that it led to a national rising against Turkey and against foreign control of the economy. Rather than allow chaos, Gladstone reluctantly ordered British land and sea forces to Egypt to restore order and impose control.

Gladstone and Gordon, 1885

The great problem with taking territory is that one thing leads to another. Having taken Egypt and installed Evelyn Baring (later Lord Cromer) as Consul General, it then became necessary to secure its southern neighbour, the huge area of the Sudan, which was under the authority of Egypt. In many respects the Sudan was in a worse state of misgovernment and turmoil than Egypt. Of particular importance was a Sudanese resistance movement which was determined to break free from Egyptian control. Just at the time the British moved into Egypt, this resistance movement came under the leadership of Mohammed Abdullah, who took the title 'the Mahdi' – 'the chosen one of the Prophet'. The British press of the day tended to dismiss him as 'the mad Mahdi', but whatever the nature of his religious views he was an inspiring and formidable leader. His army overran large parts of the Sudan.

To contain him, Gladstone's government sent a force to the region under the popular Victorian military hero, General Gordon, known as 'Chinese Gordon' because of his adventures on behalf of the Qing dynasty in crushing the Taiping rebellion. There was doubt and controversy over what Gordon's exact instructions were and whether he ignored them. Had he been asked to lead an orderly retreat from the Sudan or stay and fight? Gordon was a brave and able soldier, but he was very much his own man; he had a way of interpreting orders to make them fit his own plans, which made him very difficult to work with. Like the Mahdi, he had developed his own intensely held religious beliefs. A committed evangelical Christian, he seems to have believed that he had a calling from God to stay in the

Sudan to fight the Mahdi. This was a replay of the Crusades. He declined to withdraw.

It was believed by many in Britain that Gladstone, irritated by Gordon's refusal to follow orders, deliberately delayed sending a relief army when Gordon became besieged in Khartoum by the Mahdi's army of Dervish warriors. When Gladstone did eventually authorize the dispatch of a force, it arrived two days too late; Gordon had already been killed on 5 January 1885. An angered Queen Victoria let it be known publicly that she regarded Gladstone as being largely responsible for the tragedy. The Prime Minister was jeered and hissed at by crowds in Downing Street for allowing a hero to be martyred.

Omdurman, 1898

The Mahdi died of typhus six months later but his struggle went on. The climax came a little over a decade later. Determined to gain mastery in the Sudan, which it had evacuated after Gordon's death, Britain sent a fully prepared army under Herbert Kitchener to take on the Dervishes. Cromer's skilful administration of Egypt, which included the building of railways into the Sudan, made possible the highly effective British military operations that Kitchener mounted. The final overwhelming victory came in 1898 with the defeat of the Dervishes in the battle of Omdurman. This secured Anglo-Egyptian sovereignty in the Sudan.

The Fashoda incident, 1899

France, Britain's great imperial rival in the region was not pleased. The French argued that the Sudan was still unclaimed territory and, therefore, fully open to them. Only a few days after his success at Omdurman, Kitchener came face to face with a French expeditionary force under General Marchand at Fashoda, a Sudanese town on the Upper Nile. War seemed to threaten, but after a courteous if tense exchange, Marchand, on instructions from Paris, gave ground and withdrew. Eventually, in March 1899, France signed an agreement recognizing Anglo-Egyptian supremacy in the Sudan. War was soon to come for the British in Africa but when it did it was not in the north against France but in the south against the Boers.

Growing tensions in South Africa

Cape Colony in southern Africa had been taken from the Dutch at the end of the eighteenth century. Although this British seizure was formally sanctioned at the Congress of Vienna in 1815, friction remained between the British and Dutch (Boer) settlers. Cape Colony was granted self-government in 1872. Natal, which had been largely Zulu territory, was annexed by Britain in 1843 and was also given self-government in 1872. The Convention of Bloemfontein in 1854 recognized the Transvaal and the Orange Free State as independent Dutch republics, but it left a dangerous situation. The British and Dutch settlers regarded each other with hostility and both were resented by the native African peoples who had been forced off their land by the Europeans.

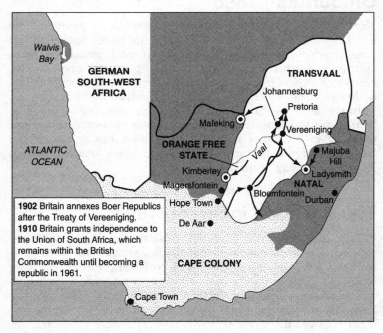

Figure 22 the Anglo-Boer war, 1899–1902

Fighting broke out between the British and the Boers in 1880, ending with a British defeat at Majuba Hill in 1881. This led to the London Convention in 1884 at which Gladstone's government accepted that southern Africa should be divided between the British in the Cape Province and Natal and the Dutch Boers (farmers) who would occupy the Transvaal and the Orange Free State. However, although Britain formally recognized Boer rights of self-government in the Transvaal, it continued to claim ambiguously that it exercised 'suzerainty' [authority] over the region.

The *Uitlanders*

One day in 1886 in a village in the Transvaal a little lad called Erasmus saw a bright shiny object on the ground. He proudly took it home to show his father, who recognized what it was – it was a piece of gold. The discovery changed the face of the Transvaal. Prospectors and traders flooded in. The violent and uncivilized behaviour of this unsavoury collection of people, was wholly unacceptable to the sober, God-fearing, Boers. *Uitlander* is Afrikaans for alien. It was the term the Boers applied to the motley newcomers, who, encouraged by the thought of rich pickings, swelled the population of the diamond and gold mining areas of the Transvaal, being especially numerous in Johannesburg. Determined to protect their way of life from being destroyed, the Boers under their President, Paul Kruger, refused to extend political or electoral rights to the intruders.

Cecil Rhodes

Relations between the Boers and Britain became increasingly strained when the British supported the *Uitlanders* in their demand for the rights of citizenship. Much of this was due to one man, Cecil Rhodes. Born in Britain in 1853, Rhodes, a fiercely self-driven man, had gone to southern Africa at the age of 17; he stayed to make a fortune in the diamond mines of Kimberley and the gold mines of Transvaal. He conceived a grand vision of a British empire in Africa which would extend the entire length of the continent from the Cape to Cairo. He was an unabashed racist who believed that 'we British are the first race in the world and the more of the world we inhabit the better it is for the human race. I would annexed the planets if I could.'

Rhodes is now seen by some as one of those Victorian men of action who denied themselves the pleasures of sex so that they could put all their energies into empire building. The argument is that they sublimated their desires. This is a fascinating Freudian thought, though suspect since it rests upon the questionable presumption that a later generation understands people better than they did themselves. But it does add spice to the concoction.

In 1885, Rhodes persuaded the British government to take over Bechuanaland (modern Botswana), to prevent the Germans seizing it. Hoping to lay hold of gold mines further north, Rhodes then tricked the chiefs of the tribes of the regions of present-day Zimbabwe and Zambia into giving up key territories, which were then incorporated in 1889 into his British South Africa Company (BSAC). With financial backing from some of the world's richest bankers, and its own private army, the BSAC became a very powerful organization. It controlled territory, held mining rights, and had the authority to raise taxes. Technically, it was under the British government but in everything that mattered it was a law unto itself. It was little surprise when Rhodes became Prime Minister of Cape Colony in 1890; his power and influence seemed limitless.

But if his dream of a southern Africa totally controlled by Britain was to come true, Rhodes knew that the power of the Boers would have to be broken. Since they would not willingly give way, he was quite prepared to contemplate war. Conflict became a certainty after 1895 when Joseph Chamberlain, a man with as intense a belief in Britain's imperial destiny as Rhodes', was appointed Colonial Secretary.

The Jameson raid, 1895

Rhodes was determined to use the *Uitlander* issue to overthrow the Boers. At his instigation, Dr Starr Jameson, the chief administrator of Rhodes' Chartered Company of South Africa, led a group of 500 men into the Transvaal hoping to stimulate a full-scale rising against Kruger's government. The raid proved a botched affair. Jameson's force were captured and he and the ringleaders were ignominiously sent to London for trial. Rhodes resigned as Prime Minister and Anglo-Boer relations were further soured. The Boers suspected with good reason that Chamberlain had had prior knowledge of the raid and had given it his full backing.

The role of Joseph Chamberlain

Chamberlain was looking for a war. He took up the cause of the British in the Transvaal, claiming that they were entitled to full constitutional rights. This the Boers resolutely refused to consider, which was exactly what Chamberlain had hoped for. As indicated by his involvement in the Jameson Raid, he was spoiling for a fight. Chamberlain's secret correspondence with Alfred Milner, whom he appointed in 1897 as the High Commissioner in the Cape, shows beyond doubt that his deliberate aim was to manoeuvre the Boers into a position where they had no recourse but to fight. Indeed Chamberlain had selected Milner knowing full well that the Commissioner's unstable temperament and total belief in the supremacy of British claims in southern Africa would make the breakdown of negotiations with the Boers inevitable. In 1899, Kruger, exasperated by Britain's unreasonable demands, as put by Milner, abandoned any further talks. In October, the two Boer republics declared war on Britain, a war that was to last for three years.

The skullduggery of Rhodes, Milner and Chamberlain had certainly made war likely, but what made it unavoidable was the basic question which had been there since the Boers and the British first settled in the region. Who was to run South Africa? Who was to have the final authority? Was southern Africa to be a British dominion or a Boer republic? Beneath the dispute about the rights of the *Uitlanders* was the matter of sovereignty. As Kruger said to Milner during the final talks at Bloemfontein before war broke out, 'it is our country you want'. For Chamberlain, British supremacy in the region was necessary in order to maintain Britain's strength as an imperial power; he regarded South Africa before 1899 as the weakest link in the chain of the empire.

Chamberlain's plans for the empire

To appreciate why Chamberlain was prepared to go to war over all this, his particular attitude has to be grasped. Chamberlain had a dream, a vision of the empire becoming a unique, worldwide, economic union of states under the leadership of Britain. Such a union, he believed, would solve all Britain's financial problems at home. The money that would flow in as a result of preferential trade with the colonies would enable the nation to solve the problems of poverty and social inequality which industrialization had brought to Victorian and Edwardian Britain. Unless such a scheme as his was adopted, the result would be class war, since the only alternative left to governments would be to resort to crippling taxation of the rich. In pushing these ideas, Chamberlain called for an end to free trade, the tradition by which Britain had operated for generations and which was associated in many minds with the days of Britain's greatness as the 'workshop of the world'. He claimed those days had gone. By the end of the nineteenth century, Britain was locked in economic struggle with competitors who were fast overtaking her. The answer was to abandon free trade and adopt imperial preference.

In the end his dreams went unrealized; the empire never developed in the way he wanted. But Chamberlain left his mark; in the decades before his death in 1914 he had introduced into Britain the most divisive domestic issue of the age, the furious battle between free trade and protection.

The Boer War, 1899–1902

The war lasted for three years, and 400,000 British troops, including Australian, Canadian and New Zealand contingents were used. After much effort and many reverses, Britain's superiority in numbers and weaponry finally wore down the Boer guerrillas and forced their surrender. From the beginning there was a significant group in Britain who were deeply unhappy with the war. Referred to as 'pro-Boers', they questioned the morality of Britain's position. Initially, however, the war was widely popular in Britain. Such events as the relief of Mafeking which saw the end of a prolonged Boer siege produced great public rejoicing. The Conservative government deliberately played upon the patriotism of the electorate in 1900 by calling and comfortably winning what became known as the 'Khaki election'.

Yet, six years later it suffered a landslide defeat at the hands of the Liberals. Part of the reason for the serious falling away of support for the Conservative government was its dismal record in the Boer War. The pro-Boers drew constant attention to the failure of British forces to win the war quickly. Still more disturbing to the government were the reports of the extreme measures which the British forces employed in trying to break Boer resistance. The most notorious of these was the internment of civilians in 'concentration camps', where the cramped conditions and poor food frequently led to the spread of fatal diseases. Some 28,000 Boer women and children died in the camps, mainly from typhus and cholera.

The deaths were the result of bad organization, not deliberate planning. Nevertheless, the Liberals accused the government of employing 'the methods of barbarism'. Another Liberal, David Lloyd George, declared: 'we have now taken to killing babies'. Not only did its disastrous strategy against Boer civilians prove an international scandal; the fact that it took the might of the British imperial army three long years to overcome an outnumbered group of farmers caused embarrassment at home and aroused ridicule abroad.

The fighting was finally ended in May 1902 by the Peace of Vereeniging. Under its terms, the Boer republics were absorbed into the British empire but with the promise that they would eventually be granted independence. The commitment was honoured in 1907 when the two states became self-governing colonies. The Boers were sufficiently reconciled to the situation to enter the Union of South Africa in 1910.

However, the Union constitution did not settle the issue of the rights of the native Africans. Although their right to vote was recognized in the Cape, it was denied them elsewhere in the Union. This injustice was to become a critical issue in the following decades.

The growth of African nationalism

On the eve of European colonization in the 1870s there had been some 800 tribal or regional units in Africa. Imperialism may have been a mixed blessing for the Africans but one effect was the creation of definite geographical and political structures. These were often arbitrary but they had the result, not looked for by the colonizing powers, of establishing a concept of African nationhood.

Given the wide differences among the peoples of sub-Saharan Africa, this concept did not grow at a consistent pace and it was never the intention of the European administrators to encourage its development. The aim of the colonial nations during the period of the scramble for Africa 1870–1914, was to gain territory at the expense of their rivals, not to stimulate African nationalism. Nevertheless, it was the colonialists' own policies that had led, by 1914, to the formation of over 40 distinct areas that were to become the future nations of Africa.

In the decades after 1918, the pace of nationalism quickened. The Great War, in which many Africans had played a conspicuous part had, according to the Allied Powers, been fought to make the world 'safe for democracy'. Self-determination and the right of all peoples to be free were principles enunciated in the League of Nations Charter; they could not now be denied to the African. The terms of the mandates applying to the colonies taken from Germany at Versailles clearly implied that the newly governed territories were to be administered in the interests of the native population. The colonial overlords in Africa were reluctant to admit all this and continued to develop their territories without regard to awakening African aspirations. The colonizers still thought in terms of tribal units and regions linked together solely by their dependence upon colonial patronage.

Initially the African leaders had given good reason for their masters to think in this way; seeking preferment for themselves, they had tended not to challenge the attitudes of their overlords. Indeed the African response, excluding those Muslim areas which coincided historically with regions of Arab settlement, was to imitate the lifestyle of the Europeans. The temptation for the ambitious African in regard to dress, religion and education was to copy the European example. The power of this impulse was expressed by a native Tanganyikan in 1925: 'To the African mind to imitate Europeans is civilization.'

It should be stressed that, for the great majority of Africans in tropical Africa, their main point of contact with the Europeans was the Christian missionary. African adherence to western missionary churches was widespread; significantly, this was an area where Africans could accommodate to western ways without entirely abandoning local beliefs and customs. The first sign of genuine African independence came with this ability to accept the new order by adapting it to the known ways. This would in time create tension, as subsequent religious divisions in Uganda and Kenya were to show, but in the inter-war years religion was an important factor encouraging African awareness.

West Africa

The strictly political African organizations were few in number but in the post-Versailles atmosphere they were to become increasingly influential. Based on a nineteenth-century Gold

Coast native organization, a National Congress of British West Africa was set up; this drew members from Nigeria, Gambia, Sierra Leone and the Gold Coast. Urged on by African-Americans like W.E.B. Du Bois, who were beginning to explore their African roots, there were attempts to develop a pan-African consciousness. The fragmented nature of Africa politically made it difficult for pan-Africanism to gain ground and no universal African organization came into being. As yet African consciousness was confined to its separate regions.

Yet, considerable headway was made in West Africa. Nigerian students returned from being educated in Britain and America claiming 'Africa for the Africans' and 'autonomy for Nigeria within the British Empire'. Novel though these slogans sounded, they expressed a wish to advance towards greater freedom essentially in accord with the ideology of the imperial power. This attitude was even more apparent in the French African territories. French colonial policy had always been more centralized than the British and even when, as in Senegal, pro-African socialist movements grew up, their aim was the advancement of the African to full equality within the French imperial system, not in opposition to it.

South Africa

A similar picture presented itself in southern Africa. In 1925 a Zulu-led South African National Congress was formed. Despite its name, this organization, while making a stand against the more oppressive race laws, was unable to achieve widespread backing from the black races. Asian groups achieved more success through their Natal Indian Congress, formed as early as the 1890s by Mohandas Gandhi, as their representative body.

East Africa

In eastern parts of the continent there was an equivalent East African Association which similarly derived its support from a variety of colonial territories. The problem for the East Africans tended to be greater. They lacked the educational opportunities of their west coast brothers and unlike them had no representatives in the local councils and parliaments. This reflected an important feature of colonial history. Where the European settlers were numerous and strongly established, as in southern and eastern Africa and in the Belgian Congo, it was invariably more difficult for the politically ambitious or nationalistically-minded African to progress. North and South Rhodesia were further British examples of this.

Weaknesses of the African nationalist movement

A basic weakness for nationalists in such areas was the lack of a broad popular following. For the most part, the native Africans were poorly educated members of a peasant community; it needed time before they would become responsive to the attraction of nationalism. Notwithstanding these limitations, the raw material was there. Money as a form of exchange became better understood and this in turn produced a cash crop economy; an industrial labour force developed in the towns. These were trends of obvious political significance and would be turned to account by those leaders and movements who wanted the African to take his destiny into his own hands. But for the moment the politically active African aimed at winning concessions from his imperial master rather than challenging an alien rule.

The period before 1939 is not at first sight a dramatic one but it was significant. An identifiable shape to African nationalism was emerging; native politicians were gaining experience, organizations were forming, and the ideology of change was being analyzed. What was needed was something dramatic and graphic to inspire the African to turn potential for change into actuality. Such drama was soon to be provided by the Second World War which, avowedly fought as a struggle for freedom against subjugation, dealt the death blow to imperialism. This, together with the graphic triumph of Indian nationalism against British rule in India, gave Africa a drive towards independence that within a generation would prove irresistible.

09 the struggle for Indian independence

This chapter will cover:
- the growth of the Indian nationalist movement
- the Amritsar massacre
- the impact of the world wars on India
- the role of Gandhi
- the gaining of independence
- the end of the Raj.

The Indian mutiny in the middle of the nineteenth century and the colonial race between the European powers for colonies in the years from 1870 to 1914 strengthened Britain's resolve to remain in the sub-continent. However, nationalism, a potent force in the rise of European imperialism, also inspired powerful feelings of independence among many Indians. As in so many areas where colonialism spread, it carried with it the seeds of its own eventual destruction. By the end of the nineteenth century, it was evident that the Indian desire for freedom would prove increasingly difficult for Britain to contain.

The British Raj responsible for governing India was made up of remarkably thin human resources. Although British officials dominated the key posts in the civil service, barely 1 per cent of the civilian population was British; similarly the Indian army, while officered by the British, was composed overwhelmingly of native Indians. Burdening the British administration and weakening the organization of Indian nationalism was the complex nature of Indian society. Made up of varying and often conflicting races, castes and religions, India had no single nationalist voice. Until some semblance of unity could be achieved, Indian aspirations would be frustrated. Not surprisingly this frustration found outlet in increasing violence. This began to mount after the haughty but efficient Viceroy, Lord Curzon, left India in 1910.

Shaken by disturbances and unrest throughout the sub-continent, but particularly in Bengal, the British government made some concession to the demand for a greater share by Indians in local affairs. But this was no longer sufficient; the total withdrawal of British rule was now the aim of nationalists. The relationship between Hindus and Muslims complicated matters at this point. The latter, outnumbered by three to one by the former, found it expedient to co-operate with the British in the hope of gaining special minority safeguards. Resenting this, the Hindus became the most extreme group opposing British control. By the time the First World War intervened it was clear that the future of British authority over India was highly problematic.

The First World War itself was of considerable significance to the Indian question. Not only did it give India an opportunity to contribute to the Allied cause with over a million Indians fighting on the various fronts, but it also provided a great moral stimulus to the independence movement. The Western allies claimed to have fought the war to uphold the principles of democracy and national self-determination. If that indeed was the case, the nationalists pointedly asked, did it not follow that Britain should withdraw from India if that is what the Indian people wanted?

In Britain itself political opinion over India had become deeply divided by the end of the war. Such controversy was increased when news of events in Amritsar in April 1919 came through.

The Amritsar massacre, 1919

Jallianwalla in Amritsar, the Sikh holy city, formed a rough square of hard earth, walled in on all sides by a series of close packed houses. On 13 April 1919, a crowd of 20,000 Hindus, including woman and children, gathered in the square to protest against their subjection to Britain's rule. They were noisy but unarmed and not particularly threatening. However, Brigadier-General Reginald Dyer, the British officer responsible for keeping order, was unhappy and edgy. Only two days before, an English woman missionary had been attacked and knocked unconscious by a mob. Quick-tempered and brusque, Dyer was not prepared to be patient. He had previously announced a ban on public meetings. Now, without giving the crowd a chance to disperse, he ordered his Indian troops to open fire with rifles and machine guns. Hemmed in on all sides there was no way of escape. In the mayhem that followed 379 protesters were killed and another 1,500 injured.

If one incident could be said to have doomed British rule in India, then the Amritsar massacre was it. It was not simply that it intensified Indian nationalism, turning moderates into revolutionaries. What was especially significant was the reaction in Britain. Even Winston Churchill, an ardent believer in Britain's right and duty to govern India, was appalled. He described the event as an act of 'frightfulness', a word he chose with great care since it had been the term applied to German atrocities in the 1914–18 war. He explained in the House of Commons: 'What I mean by frightfulness is the inflicting of great slaughter or massacre upon a particular crowd of people, with the intention of terrorising not merely the rest of the crowd, but the whole district or country.'

Churchill added that although it was a monstrous incident it stood in 'sinister isolation'. He was trying to convince his hearers that such actions were neither condoned by the British authorities nor typical of the character of British rule. This was unconvincing to those who believed that India could be kept a British possession only by the use of unacceptable military force. Edwin Montagu, the Secretary of State for India, asked rhetorically, 'Are you going to keep your hold upon India by terrorism, racial humiliation and subordination?' He had in mind the infamous 'crawling order' issued by Dyer that required any Indians who wished to pass along the street where the missionary had been assaulted to do so on their hands and knees.

At a hastily-convened court of inquiry in India, Dyer proved unrepentant. He revealed that his actions had been in line with the instructions he had received from his superiors: 'No gatherings of persons nor processions of any sort will be allowed. All gatherings will be fired on.' Dyer admitted that he had, indeed, intended to terrorize the Indian people. To save further scandal, Dyer was retired from the army on grounds of ill health and sent back to England.

Reactions to Amritsar in Britain and India

Yet in spite of the revelations of Dyer's deliberate severity, there were some in England who were ready to defend him. A fund was even set up for him. Those who contributed were those who believed that the defence of the Raj justified the use of tough measures, regrettable though they might sometimes be, as in this case. But the tide was turning against such views. They simply did not fit the times. What the Amritsar massacre had done was to polarize attitudes in Britain. The First World War had been fought to make the world safe for democracy. Moreover, 1919, the year of Amritsar, was the year the war formally ended with the signing of the Treaty of Versailles, whose redrawing of the map of the world was based on the principle of the right of self-determination. It made little moral or political sense for Britain, one of the major victor nations and therefore pledged to that principle, to continue ruling the peoples of the empire against their will. It was the realization of this that turned British thinking towards the idea of self-rule for India and the advanced colonies.

Some, such as Churchill, would resist until the end, but a process had been set in motion. Once any system of government begins to doubt its right to control, its days are numbered. The days of empire were drawing to a close. It would take time, of course, and there would be many problems along the way, but a significant change in the character of the British empire was underway.

Amritsar also showed the sharp divisions among the Indian people themselves. The victims of the massacre had been largely Hindus. Far from condemning the killings, therefore, the Sikhs of Amritsar went through with a ceremony in their Golden Temple in which they installed Dyer as an 'honorary Sikh'. Such apparent cynicism was an example of the great religious divide in the sub-continent between Hindus, Sikhs and Muslims, a bitter and lethal divide that would blight the history of Indian independence. Yet, fascinatingly, it was to be non-violence that now became the chief factor in the advance of Indian nationalism and this largely because of one man.

Gandhi

In 1931, journalists and press photographers were intrigued by a particular Indian nationalist who came to London to attend a round table conference on the future of India. He did not appear very impressive, this short-sighted, emaciated Hindu, dressed untidily in a homespun dhoti and shawl and leaning on a staff whose thickness emphasized the thinness of his body. Yet this skeletal figure was Mohandas Gandhi, known to his followers as Mahatma – 'great soul'. This was the man who would bring an end to British rule in India, and who, in doing so, would begin the process by which the empire itself would be abandoned.

As an Indian nationalist leader, Gandhi had suffered insult, beatings and imprisonment. To these hurts he added his own suffering by engaging in a series of public fasts. His purpose in starving himself was two-fold: to rebuke his followers for their failings and to embarrass the British. He knew that his non-violent, passive resistance would stump the officials of the Raj. They had not met this sort of protest before. Rioters were easy to deal with; handling a saint was a much harder proposition.

Born in 1869, Mohandas Karamchand Gandhi had trained in London as a lawyer. He had then gone to South Africa to organize passive resistance to the anti-Black race laws which operated in the Transvaal. In 1915, he returned to his own country intent on using the same techniques to undermine the

British hold on India. Beyond doubt Gandhi was the single most important influence in the growth of Indian nationalism. A devout Hindu, he nonetheless sought mutual respect and tolerance between all religions and social castes. His simple, devout lifestyle appealed hugely to the great mass of the Indian peasantry. He wished to identify with all castes, even the 'untouchables' – those regarded as the lowest form of humanity. Thousands flocked to gain a glimpse of him, particularly during his famous public fasts. Protecting him from his enthusiastic followers required a large army of minders. Someone once remarked on how expensive it was to keep Gandhi in poverty.

Within a few years, Gandhi had awakened the hitherto unpoliticized Indians. The fragmented regions began to unite against the British presence. For a time he was even able to gain Muslim support. When, in the early 1920s, Britain was on the verge of war with Muslim Turkey, Gandhi played upon the fears of Indian Muslims and brought them over to his side.

In the twenties and thirties Gandhi's concept of non-violent civil disobedience was adopted nationwide as the principle instrument with which to embarrass British officialdom. The most famous example of this was the 'salt protest' of 1930 when collecting tens of thousands along the way he led a march covering nearly 250 miles to the coastal town of Dandi. There he picked up a lump of salt from the beach and crushed it in his hands. It was a simple but hugely symbolic gesture. Salt was an essential food preservative used by all Indians. Gandhi was protesting against the way the people were not allowed to gather natural sea salt but were forced to buy the heavily taxed government-owned variety. For this he was arrested and imprisoned, as he was on three other separate occasions, but this served only to enhance his veneration among ordinary Indians.

However, it was not the ordinary Indians but the politicians who were to determine India's fate. Gandhi's simple philosophy did not always attract the educated Indian any more than it did the activists, who became impatient with passive resistance. Those who believed that India's way ahead lay in urbanization and industrialization had little time for Gandhi's quaint vision of a village, cottage-industry based India. Furthermore, his wish to embrace the 'untouchables' seemed, to sophisticated Indians, to portend dangerous, social revolution. Nor did Gandhi's hopes of Hindu-Muslim harmony survive long. Fearing that independence attained on Gandhian terms would lead to their subjection to the Hindu majority, the Muslim nationalists preferred separate to collective action. The riots and disturbances which marred India between 1919 and 1947 were not exclusively anti-British; they were often expressions of intense Hindu-Muslim rivalry.

In the face of communal disorder, the British tried to ease tensions by a number of concessions, such as the India Act of 1935, which offered local self-government. But it was too late for these policies. India could not now be satisfied with anything less than complete independence. For the nationalists, it was not a question of whether Britain should withdraw, simply one of when. But what must be stressed is that at no time in the 100 years before Independence in 1947 could Britain have imposed herself on India had the majority of Indians opposed it. A fact pointed out by modern Indian historians is that the British Raj was a form of partnership which required the co-operation of the Indian people for it to work. The figures make this plain; in the last century of the British rule of India, the population of over 400 million was governed by merely 1,000 British civil servants. The rest of the governing classes were all native Indians.

India and the Second World War

For a second time, world war fundamentally altered the Indian problem. As she had in 1914, Britain, with scant consultation, committed India to war. The early humiliations suffered by British forces at the hands of the Japanese appeared to presage the collapse of Britain's power east of Suez. Seizing the moment the Indian nationalists re-doubled their attacks; in 1942, the worse year of the war for the British, Gandhi inaugurated the 'Quit India' movement. The familiar round of violence and reprisals followed with misery worsened by a famine in Bengal. The native police and army remained loyal and British control was unbroken but at the cost of many lives and more political repression. Chandra Bose, an admirer of both Hitler and Japan, raised an Indian National Army to fight on the Japanese side as a means of destroying British power in India. Bose was opposed by Gandhi, and the Congress Party and his army, some 20,000 strong it was claimed, did little on the military front. Nevertheless its existence showed the degree of anti-British feeling in India.

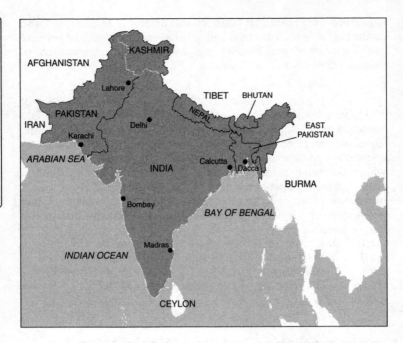

Figure 23 the division of the sub-continent at the time of independence in 1947

Indian independence, 1947

At the close of the Japanese war it was clear that to retain India against the wish of its peoples would stretch Britain's resources to breaking point. Moreover, the will to do so had largely gone. The Labour Party came into power in 1945 fully committed to independence for India. The problem was when and how this could be best arranged. The Muslim League, led by Mohammed Jinnah, was increasingly suspicious of the Hindus, represented by the Congress Party and its leader Pandit Nehru. A sizeable Sikh minority was equally apprehensive of being swamped in an independent India. To such groups, federation within a single sovereign state was not acceptable, although it had been proposed a number of times previously and was again suggested by the Labour government's representative, Stafford Cripps.

Eager now to be rid of the Indian burden, the British dispatched Earl Mountbatten as special envoy to negotiate Britain's final withdrawal. Given the reluctance of the parties concerned to consider federation, partition seemed the only solution. After much haggling, Hindu Congress and Muslim League agreed to the Mountbatten proposals: India, the sub-continent, was to be divided into two distinct states: India, overwhelmingly Hindu; Pakistan, predominantly Muslim. The Indian princes would give up their rule in return for the freedom to retain their wealth. The date for the formal end of British rule was brought forward from 1948 to 1947.

Post independence problems

This compromise was doubtless the best solution that could be arrived at, but how far it was from being a lasting one was soon revealed by the tragedy that ensued. Jinnah and the League resented having had to settle for a 'moth-eaten' Pakistan; Congress was dismayed at seeing India broken up, while the Sikhs, not being in a majority in any single region, were resolved to resist subjection in whichever of the new states they found themselves. Civil war broke out in the same week of the transfer of power from Britain. Muslim-Hindu-Sikh passions spilled over into desperate acts of mutual violence.

The independence of India had thus come at a terrible price. The creation of the separate states of India and Pakistan led to a massive cross migration of refugees: Muslims from India into Pakistan, Hindus and Sikhs from Pakistan into India. The communal riots and massacres that accompanied all this resulted in the killing of over 3 million men, women and children, 1 million dying in the Punjab alone.

India and Pakistan after independence

It has always been misleading to think of the Indian sub-continent as one country. If all the varying religions, castes, languages and systems are taken into account, India provides a more fragmented image than Europe. Even within the identifiable groups there was further diversity. The assassination of the great Hindu leader, Gandhi, by a Hindu fanatic in 1948 is a reminder of the kaleidoscopic nature of Indian politics. This is a dimension which needs to be stressed when examining post-independence India.

Effects of compromise

The fundamental flaw in the process by which India became independent in 1947 was that it was a compromise. As the mass migrations and communal violence showed, the partition between India and Pakistan was not a settlement. Partition simply formalized the deep division between Hindu and Muslim, leaving neither community content and infuriating large minority groups, such as the Sikhs, who were not party to the deliberations. In 1947 it was recognized that Hindus and Muslims were not prepared to contemplate peaceful co-existence in a federal state. The speed of British withdrawal obliged them to admit the reality of this divide.

From the beginning Pakistan, although gaining separation from India, felt she had got the worst of the territorial settlement. In addition, Pakistan considered she had done less well in regard to her colonial inheritance; governmental and administrative structures were not as well established as in India.

Despite the large-scale transmigrations around the time of independence, involving the movement of some 20 million people, significant disaffected minorities were left in what they regarded as occupied territories. The Punjab and Bengal were typical of such regions. Both India and Pakistan were confronted by angry, unco-operative minorities within their borders.

Poverty

A problem common to both states as they struggled to establish themselves was the endemic poverty that afflicted their rapidly growing populations. The rivalry between India and Pakistan has to be viewed against the demographic pressures on young states attempting to industrialize and modernize. Recurrent famines in the decades after independence increased communal tensions and blighted hopes of an easy transition to nationhood.

The outstanding dispute between India and Pakistan created by the partition of 1947 was over Kashmir. This had been one of the princely states in the days of the Raj; following independence India sought a takeover of the area. Kashmir, predominantly Muslim though ruled by a Hindu Maharajah, strenuously resisted and demanded union with Pakistan. The dispute reached the UN which tried to mediate. India refused to co-operate and declined to hold a referendum in Kashmir.

Border conflicts and rival claims over water sources meant that tensions persisted.

A complicating factor was the lack of unity among the Muslims themselves. This showed itself most clearly in 1972 when East Pakistan formally declared itself independent of its Western counterpart and announced the creation of the state of Bangladesh. Not unnaturally India approved of this division in the Muslim ranks and offered patronage and protection to Bangladesh. However, such was the complexity of politics in the sub-continent, that within a few years the dire poverty of the new state had produced mounting internal violence and a rejection of India's protective role.

At the time of independence it had been the declared intention of Nehru and the ruling Congress Party that India should develop as a democratic, non-aligned state. Even in the 1960s, when India found herself at war with China over disputed territory, Nehru still endeavoured to court the favour of both the Soviet Union and the USA. The strains of war and of population growth obliged the Indian Government to curtail certain political and social freedoms. These totalitarian tendencies were interpreted by observers inside and outside India as evidence of the fragility of the constitutional forms adopted in 1947. Critics suggested that authoritarianism and the caste system, though formally abandoned, were powerful Indian traditions whose effects had not died simply with the 1947 declarations of equality and democracy.

Authoritarianism was still more marked in Pakistan. Whereas India was an avowedly democratic, secular state, Pakistan, from its inception, had been a confessedly Islamic nation. Her Muslim leaders had little trust in representative government; by the late 1950s authority in Pakistan had been taken into the hands of the military who defined their control in terms of 'guided democracy'. The pressing need for land reform, the hostility of her neighbours and desperate state of the economy were the justification, argued the generals, for Pakistan's centralized control.

The Indian sub-continent had never been a united area politically, socially or nationally. At the height of the power of the British Raj, governmental control had been only partial. Notwithstanding the long nationalist struggle, independence came in 1947 at a much earlier date than had been anticipated. The euphoria that accompanied it could not long hide the deep fissures that divided India. Religion, caste, regionalism and class were the causes of separation. Compounding these was the ever-increasing demographic problem which threatened to destroy the ambitions of politicians and parties to solve the basic issue of poverty.

The independence of India in 1947 was undeniably the triumph of a particular brand of idealism, but it was an idealism that took little account of the regional, political, religious and economic realities. From the moment of their creation, India and Pakistan were to be laden with problems which were still not fully resolved at the beginning of the twenty-first century.

10

colonial Africa – missionaries and administrators

This chapter will cover:
- the contribution of the missions
- David Livingstone's explorations
- styles of colonial adminstration
- the creation of the British Commonwealth.

18 April 1874, the date his body reached England on the steamer *Malwa*, was declared to be a day of national mourning. Dr David Livingstone had come home.

Not all colonizers were driven by thoughts of wealth, status or military adventure. There were some whose chief motivation was their sense of duty to their fellow men. Prominent among these were the missionaries, men and women of faith who believed that God called them to service among native peoples in far off lands. The work was invariably arduous, exhausting and rarely spectacularly successful.

The missionaries were often a product of that special brand of religious fervour known as evangelicalism, a conviction that the performing of good works was an essential part of Christian life. Evangelicals took to heart such texts as 'inasmuch as you do this unto the least of my brethren you do it unto me' and showed their love of God by serving God's creatures on earth. In England, evangelicals became social reformers; abroad they became missionaries bringing enlightenment to the heathen. Their principal aim was to convert, but they soon learned that mere preaching would have minimal effect; they had to be very practical people. Example was paramount. So with their bibles they brought a variety of items to help the people they were seeking to persuade – needles and cotton, simple medicines and cures. Willy-nilly, they became amateur nurses and doctors and handymen. The shrewdest amongst them adapted their teaching in such a way that it incorporated rather than challenged local customs and beliefs.

David Livingstone

Someone who quickly grasped that sympathy was better than dogmatism and respect more fruitful than fear was the outstanding missionary of the Victorian era – David Livingstone. Born in Scotland in 1813 he had a hard young life. At the age of ten he went to work for 12 hours a day in the local cotton mill. Yet he still found time to study, eventually qualifying as a doctor after training at a London hospital, which he sometimes walked from his lodgings and back, a round trip of 80 kilometres (50 miles). Livingstone developed a burning conviction that he was called to the Lord's service. He joined the London Missionary Society. His first thought was to serve in China, but the Opium Wars there in the 1840s diverted him to Africa where he was to spend the greater part of his life. As with so many pioneers, no single label fits him. He was a missionary, explorer, anthropologist, anti-slaver, doctor, map-maker. His great gift was in winning the confidence of the peoples he served.

In 1840 he arrived in Cape Town and journeyed 800 kilometres (500 miles) north to Kuruman, in what became Bechuanaland. There Livingstone opened a mission and also spent time living in native villages and learning the basics of local dialects. The Africans found him an oddity at first, but his sincerity and genuine desire to understand their ways won them over. He never ridiculed their medical treatments and was quick to incorporate any practice which he found beneficial. In time, the natives came to regard him as a great healer. It was at Kuruman that two formative events took place. He was savaged by a lion and he gained a wife. In the first incident the lion bit through his shoulder muscles leaving him with a permanently disabled left arm. The second event was rather less painful but had equally lasting effects. Livingstone had been committed to the single life, believing that his missionary work left him no time for domestic bliss. However, he was won over by Mary Moffatt, the daughter of Dr Robert Moffatt, a fellow medical missionary who had first inspired him to go Africa. The marriage took place in 1845.

Mary Livingstone

Livingstone's long-suffering wife, Mary, was a Victorian heroine who deserves more credit than she usually receives. In their early married years, she went nearly everywhere with him on his exhausting journeys, as often as not travelling on a jolting bullock cart. She raised five children, all of them born within the space of five years. Eventually when things became too dangerous and exhausting, malaria being a constant threat, Livingstone decided to send his family back to England leaving him to commit himself wholly to the exploration of central Africa.

Livingstone's great expeditions

The rest of his life made him a legend in his own time and a source of wonder ever since. His first great expedition covered the years 1853–6. With only a few native bearers as companions, he made his way westward along the Zambezi river and then crossed to Luanda on the Atlantic coast. The party then retraced its steps and followed the Zambezi downstream, eventually reaching the Indian Ocean at Quelimane. Livingstone had thus crossed southern Africa from sea to sea, a distance of over 6437 kilometres (4,000 miles).

It was while making his journey eastward along the Zambezi that he became aware of an increasingly loud roaring noise. When he asked for an explanation his bearers told him it was 'the smoke that thunders'. Days later he understood their poetic reference when he became the first white man to set eyes on one of the great wonders of the natural world – the mighty falls where the Zambezi river plunged over a mile wide ledge and down a 300 feet sheer face. Awestruck by the their grandeur, he named them after Queen Victoria.

In 1856 he set out on the second of his three great explorations. Starting from the Zambezi delta he went north discovering Lake Nyasa and then Lake Tanganyika. His last great journey occupied the years 1866–73. Commissioned by the Royal Geographical Society to find the source of the Nile, he braved not only the exhausting climate and terrain of equatorial Africa, but attacks from slave traders. Britain had formally outlawed slavery in the empire in 1833 and her armies were now foremost in the abolitionist campaign to eradicate it altogether. By the time of Livingstone's explorations much of west Africa was now free of it. But in eastern and central areas the slave trade still operated. It was after coming across a party of Arab slave traders marching their African prisoners to be sold in the east coast markets, that Livingstone announced himself 'appalled by this terrible trafficking in human life'. His response was to condemn the trade as being against the law and will of God. But he did something far more practical as well. He calculated that if easier routes between the coastal region and the interior could be found this would encourage legitimate trade and so undermine slaving. It was this belief that inspired his journeys from now on. He was not simply exploring; in the name of God he was furthering the cause of the oppressed African. His term for the methods by which he tried to destroy slavery was 'commerce and Christianity'.

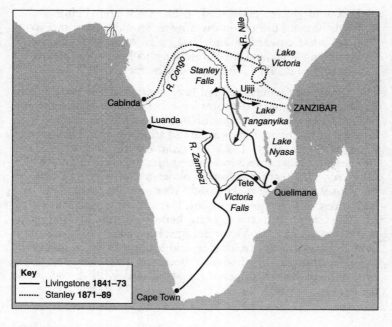

Figure 24 the major explorations of Livingstone and Stanley

Stanley

Livingstone never did find the source of the Nile. What he found were the waters of the great Congo river. It was shortly after this discovery that contact was lost with him. Interest in Livingstone was widespread in Britain and America. On his brief visits home from Africa he was feted like a modern pop star or sporting hero. When, therefore, he seemed to have disappeared into the African bush there were demands that he be found. Responding to this popular demand, the *New York Herald* sponsored a brash young journalist, Henry Morton Stanley to lead an expedition in search of Livingstone. Stanley was crude, aggressive and demanding as a leader – almost the exact opposite of the man he was sent to find – but his methods worked. Within a year of setting out from Luanda he had, by piecing together the rumours and snippets of information he picked up, located Livingstone. At Ujiji on 3 November 1871 one of the great set pieces of Victorian history took place. Stanley recorded the occasion.

I would have embraced him, only, he being an Englishman, I did not know how he would receive me; so I did what cowardice and false pride suggested was the best thing – walked deliberately up to him, took off my hat, and said: 'Dr Livingstone I presume.'

The news that Livingstone had been found excited the English-speaking world and made Stanley a hero in his own right and brought him a small fortune. Livingstone tried to continue with his travels, but by now he was an old and sick man. He died two years later in May 1873 at Ilala on the bank of Lake Tanganyika. His companions found him kneeling in an attitude of prayer. His heart was buried under a mulberry tree close to the spot where he died. His body was brought to England and laid to rest in Westminster Abbey. David Livingstone ranks with Mr Gladstone and the Queen herself as one of the great representatives of the Victorian age. Following in the tradition of such figures as Speke, Burton and Mungo Park, he had made possible, though this had not been his intention, the great explosion of British imperialism associated with the scramble for Africa.

Mary Kingsley

Mary Kingsley, well-born but bored by polite company in London drawing rooms, gave her life to Africa. She was never really a missionary – at least not in a religious sense. In fact, she said she disliked missionaries. Interestingly, she observed that Africans who had been 'civilized' by missionaries lost their true identity; they were no longer genuinely native nor fully westernized. Such views made her an embarrassment to the Colonial Office whose officials never quite knew how to handle this extraordinary woman. They were unhappy when she complained that the official administrators did not always know best when it came to handling relations with the native peoples. She referred mockingly to the Colonial Office as 'the Black Man's Burden'. When officially advised not to have dealings with the Fang tribe, whom she had befriended, she wrote, 'We belonged to the same section of the human race, with whom it is better to drink than to fight.'

In her visits back home she played, perhaps a little knowingly, the role of eccentric, which included walking around Kensington with a monkey on her shoulder. Mary gave a series of public lectures and recorded her impressions of Africa in a number of books and articles, one of whose titles indicates the range of her journeys, *Travels in West Africa, Congo Francais, Corisco and Cameroons*. Her works are still studied by scholars seeking insights into the Africa of the Victorian era.

Influenced at an early age by her much travelled father, she read and re-read the books on exploration that filled his library, and yearned to follow in his footsteps. When her parents died within six weeks of each other in 1892, she set out at the age of 30 on her first main African journey to West Africa, a region known to the Victorians as 'the white man's grave' because of the death toll its unhealthy tropical climate was reputed to cause among Europeans. She said intriguingly that she had gone to Africa to die. This may have been a tease or she may, indeed, have meant it. Her complex character and personality make her a difficult person to define precisely. In one sense she was a typical Victorian suppressed woman. Acknowledging that she was no great beauty, she seemed reconciled to spinsterhood. Her young life had been spent caring for her invalid mother. In the photographs that have survived of her she looks like the comic film character Old Mother Riley, in bombazine black dress and floral bonnet.

Yet in other ways she was extraordinarily liberated. What may have begun as a death wish became a love affair. Her work in Africa entitles her to be regarded as variously a nurse, explorer, botanist, zoologist, anthropologist, and campaigner for the rights of Africans. Although on the expeditions she went on, the bearers usually carried firearms, Mary boasted that, whatever the dangers that had come her way from man or beast, she had never fired a shot or asked others to shoot for her. She claimed to have deterred an aggressive hippopotamus by tickling its ear with the brolly she habitually carried. One of her fellow travellers, Mary Slessor, herself a woman of remarkable courage, described her namesake as 'a series of surprises, each one tenderer and more surprising than the foregoing'.

Self-assured in company, Mary Kingsley mixed easily with the rough diamonds and adventurers she travelled with, claiming that these 'palm oil ruffians' were far less of a danger than the drunken rowdies back home who plagued the streets of London. Mary financed her trips by buying and selling. She carried finished cloth with her which she bartered for local items such as rubber and ivory. She proved an excellent negotiator and peace-maker. There was an occasion when she used her remarkable strength of personality to dissuade tribal chiefs from executing prisoners. She refused to exchange her women's skirts for the comfort of male dress, saying that she would rather die on the scaffold. She once claimed, indeed, that she had survived a fall into a deep spiked animal trap only because her voluminous clothes prevented the spikes from impaling her, a protection that mere 'masculine garments' would never have afforded.

It was fitting and typical of her sense of self-sacrifice that she died in 1900 from typhoid, a disease picked up while nursing Boer prisoners during the Boer War. A month after her death, in a touchingly appropriate tribute to her, a meeting was held at her old home in Kensington to inaugurate the African Society, an organization dedicated to the study of the peoples and geography of that continent.

Styles of administration

In 1800 the only British possessions in Africa had been a few scattered forts on the west coast. Yet by 1900, Britain was in possession of large areas of the continent stretching from Egypt to the Cape. Although there was constant tension between the powers during the scramble for Africa and particular points of friction, there was no open war. This is partly explained by the fact that at a major conference in Berlin in 1884 presided over by the German Chancellor, Bismarck, the European powers had drawn up a form of gentlemen's agreement as to how they would behave. They promised not to seize territory already claimed by another power and not to enter into secret agreements. Significantly, no Africans were invited to the conference. While the agreement may have prevented war, it quickened the rush to take unclaimed territory. In the British case the way had been prepared by private charter companies which had established themselves in various parts of west and east Africa during the scramble. The Royal Niger Company was one such; formed in 1886 its purpose was to check French expansion by developing trade and claiming the right to look after native affairs. It was not until 1900 that Nigeria formally became a Crown colony under direct British administration. Other examples were the Imperial British East Africa Company, chartered in 1888, and Cecil Rhodes's own British South Africa Company, formed in 1889.

Differing colonial attitudes

Not all the colonial powers behaved in the same way towards the peoples they ruled. Whether the people were exploited or treated well varied with the European power concerned. It also depended on local conditions and the attitude of the individual administrators on the spot. Notwithstanding the excitement that imperialism aroused back home in the mother countries, in Africa itself progress was often slow and undramatic. With no time-scale of growth to work to, there was frequently a lack of urgency about colonial administration. The fight against the slave traders, who remained very active, and against disease preoccupied many of the new states. European investment in Africa was limited; it was the heavy borrowing of the administrators that brought capital into the new colonies. The railways, whose development became an impressive feature of African growth before 1914, was financed by loans.

It is worth noting how Britain differed from the other colonial power in running her colonies after 1870. In the French territories, administration was centralized and direct, the object being to assimilate the native population into the system in which they would eventually be granted full citizenship. 'The creation of black Frenchmen' was one description of this policy. Portuguese, German and Belgian colonial policy was also centralized but with far less emphasis on the training of Africans in their own administration. In contrast, in British territories indirect rule was the norm; this decentralized approach prevented any real integration between natives and colonials. Local traditions and institutions would continue, where acceptable, under the benign gaze of the British district commissioner.

Frederick Lugard

A major figure in this regard was Frederick Lugard who made 'indirect rule' his guiding principle. One the most enlightened and influential administrators in British Africa, Lugard worked in Uganda in the 1890s and in Nigeria in the early 1900s. Initially he was an agent for the charter companies. Then, when the British government formally took these over as colonies, he worked as a government official. Although he was a firm believer in the superiority of Western culture, Lugard's policy was to improve the conditions of the local people, not by imposing Western standards on them but by basing their education on their own tribal customs and ways. He urged his officials to see their essential role as being to provide technical advice and assistance.

This was well intentioned and, at its best, proved highly beneficial. But there was, of course, a danger that it might slip into simple paternalism, leaving the local population subservient and denied access to posts of genuine worth in public administration. As in India, so in some African colonies, ambitious, educated people began to resent the patronizing but restrictive hand of British colonialism.

The imperial balance sheet

By 1914 Africa had been introduced to some of the best and the worst elements of British imperialism. On the credit side, Europe had brought humanitarianism and enlightenment. Advances in communications, education, food production and medicine were undoubtedly benefits; concepts of justice and democracy, albeit not always applied in practice, were also obvious gains. The new states that Britain created were artificial structures but they did provide the basis of subsequent African nationhood. Against these gains have to be set the destruction of valuable, time-honoured, native traditions and the exploitation of the African that derived from European feelings of cultural and racial superiority. The irony was that without ever intending it, European colonialism had introduced the seeds of its own dissolution. Europe had taught Africa the language and methods of modern politics.

From empire to commonwealth

'All the empires of the past were founded on the idea of assimilation. But the British Empire does not stand for assimilation but for the richer and fuller life of the individual nations within it.' These words of Jan Smuts of South Africa, addressing a gathering of dominion prime ministers in 1917, defined the concept of the Commonwealth, an association of free and independent nations as opposed to an empire dominated by Britain. At this same 1917 meeting, a resolution was adopted calling on Britain to recognize that the dominions had developed into 'autonomous nations of an Imperial Commonwealth'. The resolution added that the widely divergent peoples of the old empire, often different in language, race, tradition and economic development, made it neither realistic nor desirable for Britain to attempt to continue running a centralized system from Westminster.

The truth of the dominions' claim was undeniable. The part played during the 1914–18 war by Canada, New Zealand, South Africa and Australia had proved beyond any lingering doubt that they were in fact equal partners with Britain. The question was how to translate that equality into a form that would preserve the traditional links with Britain. There were problems. The dominions were by no means united amongst themselves. Australia and Canada were confident of being able to go their own way but New Zealand had anxieties about coping as a sovereign state in a highly competitive world. South Africa with its memories of the Anglo-Boer War had at times a positively anti-British attitude; when the National party leader Hertzog, succeeded Smuts as Prime Minister in 1924, the signs were that South Africa might withdraw from association with Britain altogether.

A further complication was the existence of the Irish Free State, which been created by the partition in 1921 when Ireland had been divided between the Catholic south (the Free State) and the Protestant north (Ulster). The Free State had been granted dominion status; this entailed a formal allegiance to the Crown and the right of the UK to control key Irish ports. Irish nationalists resented this and the Dublin government frequently embarrassed Britain over legal and constitutional matters.

Many of these questions were discussed at a further conference of dominion ministers in 1926. A considerable measure of agreement was reached, much of the credit for which went to the conference chairman, Lord Balfour. Conscious of how important formalities can be, Balfour produced a declaration whose careful wording helped lessen the fears of the more suspicious dominions. Balfour defined the Commonwealth as 'a group of self-governing communities' and went on to stress the total autonomy of the member nations of the Commonwealth. The conference also agreed that legislation passed at Westminster should be binding in the dominions only if ratified by the parliaments of the dominion concerned.

These advances were incorporated in the Statute of Westminster of 1931, which made the parity and equality of the dominions with Britain an unchallengeable legal principle. The Statute of 1931 is rightly regarded as the charter of the new Commonwealth.

However, a major problem remained. The Statute of 1931 regulated affairs between Britain and the dominions only; it did not alter the relationship of the Britain with her colonies and dependencies. The new Commonwealth was to exist alongside the old empire. In 1931 the Commonwealth, in effect, represented 'the white man's club'. The Statute did not touch on the question of whether the dependencies would subsequently gain the same degree of freedom as the white dominions. Not unnaturally, nationalists in the colonies argued strongly that the Statute of Westminster clearly implied eventual equality and independence for all.

For Britain the stumbling block was India. Commercial, strategic and historical ties made it impossible for Britain to consider independence for India, 'the jewel in the Crown', without raising dangerous aspirations for freedom throughout the empire. India was still a potent symbol of Britain's world status. Three-quarters of the population of the entire empire were to be found in the sub-continent. If India were lost, Britain would be diminished. Such considerations could not be ignored, even though a large body of British opinion viewed concepts of this kind as having been rendered obsolete by the 1931 Statute. Indeed, by 1931, significant steps towards self-government for India had already been taken, but it would require another 16 years and the Second World War before Indian independence would be formally granted. Until that occurred, none of the non-white dependencies could make effective moves in a similar direction.

In an important area the new Commonwealth proved a major disappointment. Behind the constitutional niceties of dominion status lay a hard-headed expectation of economic gain. Unfortunately, the creation of the new Commonwealth coincided with the worldwide depression of the 1930s. Hopes for large-scale British investment in the dominions and a belief in Britain that imperial preferences would fulfil the long-standing dreams of a great international economic union, along the lines that Joseph Chamberlain had envisaged, were not realized.

In the event, therefore, the Statute of Westminster which defined the Commonwealth in 1931 was little more than the recognition of what had already happened – the growth to full independence of the white dominions. The empire, in the form of colonies and dependencies, still existed and would continue to do so until the loss of India set in motion a process that led to the abandonment of old-style imperialism and the forming of a multi-racial Commonwealth.

11

Britain's troubles in the Arab World

This chapter will cover:
- Britain's imperial ties in the Middle East
- The Iraqi and Palestinian mandates
- the Arab-Israeli conflict.

Six great empires entered the war in 1914: Germany, Austria-Hungary, Russia, Turkey, France and Britain. By 1919 only the last two had survived. But this placed burdens on the British and French. At the end of the First World War, under the League of Nations mandate system, Britain and France, as victors in the war, were asked to act as protective mandatory powers in the troubled area of the Middle East where the collapse of the Turkish empire had thrown things into turmoil. The Arab peoples wanted independence. The great question was how was this to be achieved. Would the old colonial powers accept the new ideas and demands? Britain took over the running of Mesopotamia (Iraq) and Palestine, while France became responsible for neighbouring Syria.

Britain and Iraq

The British mandate in Iraq had a happier history than the French in Syria. From the beginning the British administrators showed greater understanding of Arab nationalism than their French counterparts. In the first year of the mandate, 1920–1, Britain contributed over £23 million to the Iraqis which was more than she spent on her own health services at home. Almost immediately a civilian government was set up in Iraq to replace the military authority. Although advised by British officials, the personnel of this new government was wholly Iraqi and represented a cross-section of the Iraqi community. At local level, the same policy was followed of encouraging Iraqis to fill the administrative posts.

Amir Feisal, a hero of a recent rising against the Turks and popular with the British, was accepted as King of Iraq in 1921, following a plebiscite which voted overwhelmingly in his favour. Throughout the 1920s, co-operation between the British and the Iraqis continued. The advance of education, protection for minorities and equal opportunities were all guaranteed in a series of treaties and agreements. Britain protected Iraq's borders against rival claimants and helped suppress dissidents within the country. Sadly, this involved some pretty unpleasant methods. Air-strikes by RAF planes and even the use of poisoned gas was sanctioned by the British military and was backed by Churchill, the Secretary for War, on the grounds that the gas-bombs 'would inflict punishment upon recalcitrant natives without inflicting grave injury upon them'. In 1932, fully supported by Britain, Iraq was able to convince the mandate's commission that she was ready for the grant of full independence. In October 1932, Iraq was duly accepted as a full member of the League of Nations. An Arab nationalist commented 'Iraq owes is existence largely to the efforts and devotion of the British officials.'

Egypt

In another key Arab area, Egypt, King Fuad was installed by Britain at the end of the war to keep control of the rebel nationalist movements which had been challenging the British ever since their occupation had begun under Gladstone back in 1882. Fuad stayed true to Britain until his death in 1936, the year in which an Anglo-Egyptian treaty was signed granting British troops the right to stay in Egypt for another 20 years. This agreement was complicated by the Second World War, but eventually Britain did withdraw from the vital Canal zone in 1953 and from Egypt altogether three years later. But by then Britain had been through some very bitter experiences in the Middle East over its mandate for Palestine.

Britain and Palestine, 1917–48

In the twentieth century, Palestine, the Holy Land of biblical times, became a battle ground between Zionism and Arab nationalism. Zionism, which began as a response to growing anti-Semitism in the late nineteenth century, was a demand for the creation of a Jewish national homeland in Palestine, a return to the biblical land of Zion. Theodor Herzl, a Hungarian Jew, had convened the first Zionist Congress in 1897. In Britain the outstanding Zionist was Chaim Weizmann, destined to become the first President of Israel.

Zionism was opposed by the forces of Arab nationalism. The First World War had hastened the collapse of the tottering Turkish empire. This encouraged large numbers of Arabs in North Africa and the Near East to assert their national and regional independence, a movement not dissimilar in character from Zionism, though bitterly opposed to it. It was the extraordinary adventures of an Englishman, T. E. Lawrence, known as 'Lawrence of Arabia', a passionate and romantic supporter of the Arab cause, that helped bring the movement to the attention of the British.

The Balfour Declaration

In November 1917 Britain became deeply involved in this Arab-Zionist struggle when the Foreign Secretary, Arthur Balfour, issued a Declaration, in which he pledged British support for 'the establishment in Palestine of a national home for the Jewish people'. His aim in making that promise was to retain Jewish support for the Allies in the First World War. Almost exactly a year after the Balfour Declaration, Britain and France, keen to calm Arab anxieties produced the Anglo-French Declaration. This contained a promise to the Arab world that its desire for 'the free exercise of the initiative and choice of the indigenous populations' in shaping the future of Palestine would be honoured. As the Arabs saw it, this could apply only to them; the Jews were not indigenous, they were intruders.

In its eagerness to gain both Jewish and Arab support in the Middle East, Britain had thus given contradictory promises to the two peoples. The results of this soon became evident. Violence followed as the Arabs resisted the inflow of Jews into Palestine after the First World War ended. Under its mandate, Britain had the responsibility for overseeing Jewish immigration into the area. British forces tried to keep the peace between the two sides but found themselves caught in the middle and distrusted by both Jew and Arab. As the table indicates, Jewish immigration grew remarkably quickly in the 1920s and 1930s.

Arab and Jewish populations in Palestine

	1922	1932	1937	1940	1949
Arabs	590,000	770,000	850,000	950,000	250,000
Jews	84,000	180,000	400,000	460,000	720,000

In response to mounting Arab hostility over Palestine, a Labour government White Paper of 1930 recommended the curtailment of Jewish immigration. This resulted in Sidney Webb, who had drafted the Paper, being rounded on by Zionists as an enemy of the Jewish people, a fate that was to befall all British politicians down to Ernest Bevin who dared to suggest restrictions on Jewish immigration into Palestine.

British endeavours in the 1930s to maintain the Arab-Jewish population balance were made more difficult by events in Europe. With the onset in 1933 of the Nazi persecution of Jews in Germany, Palestine became not merely a home but a refuge. The Jews begged Britain to remove all limits on immigration. The Arabs responded by demanding that Jewish immigration be totally stopped.

Anti-British terrorism, 1945–8

Britain was in a cleft stick; whatever she did would anger one or other of the parties. In the hope of achieving a compromise, the British government announced in 1939 that Jewish immigration would end after a final quota of 75,000 had been permitted to enter. But Britain's plan was undermined by developments in occupied Europe during the Second World War. When the full horrors of the Holocaust were revealed at the end of the war, international sympathy for the Jews increased dramatically. Pressure on Britain, especially from America, to increase the immigration quotas became intense. At the same time, Jewish terrorism, led by the Irgun and the Stern Gang, increased. Fearful for their own survival, the Palestinian Arabs retaliated in kind. A bitter civil war ensued with Britain again caught in the crossfire. The assassination of the British minister, Lord Moyne, the murder of the UN representative, Count Bernadotte, and the bombing of the King David Hotel in Jerusalem were some of the more outstanding examples of the atrocities committed.

Britain withdraws

On becoming Foreign Secretary in 1945, Ernest Bevin promised that he would solve the Palestinian problem. Three years of frustration, during which he was accused both at home and abroad of being anti-Semitic disillusioned him. Despite Britain's efforts to control Jewish entry after 1945, immigration, legal and illegal, became unstoppable. The grim truth dawned on Bevin that, short of the total destruction of one of the sides, there was no way of resolving the Arab-Israeli conflict. In 1948 he announced that Britain was handing its mandate back to the UN and withdrawing from Palestine.

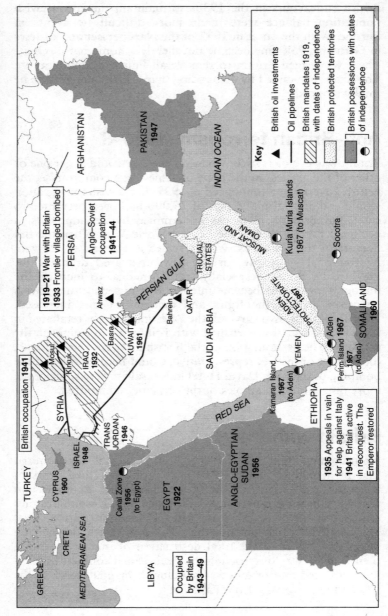

Figure 25 Britain and the Middle East, 1919–67

Key

▲ British oil investments

— Oil pipelines

▨ British mandates 1919, with dates of independence

⬚ British protected territories

◧ British possessions with dates of independence

TURKEY

GREECE

CRETE

MEDITERRANEAN SEA

CYPRUS 1960

SYRIA

ISRAEL 1948

TRANS JORDAN 1946

LIBYA

Occupied by Britain 1943–49

Canal Zone 1956 (to Egypt)

EGYPT 1922

RED SEA

ANGLO-EGYPTIAN SUDAN 1956

ETHIOPIA

1935 Appeals in vain for help against Italy 1941 Britain active in reconquest. The Emperor restored

Kamaran Island 1967 (to Aden)

YEMEN

SAUDI ARABIA

Perim Island 1967 (to Aden)

Aden 1967

ADEN PROTECTORATE 1967

SOMALILAND 1960

Socotra

Kuria Muria Islands 1967 (to Muscat)

MUSCAT AND OMAN

INDIAN OCEAN

TRUCIAL STATES

QATAR

Bahrein

KUWAIT 1961

PERSIAN GULF

Basra ▲

Ahwaz ▲

IRAQ 1932

Mosul ▲ Kirkuk ▲

British occupation 1941

PERSIA

1919–21 War with Britain 1933 Frontier villaged bombed

Anglo-Soviet occupation 1941–44

AFGHANISTAN

PAKISTAN 1947

On the very day that Britain withdrew in 1948, jubilant Zionists declared the new state of Israel. Jewish ecstasy was balanced by the searing anger of the Arab world which, believing it had been betrayed, pledged itself to the destruction of the new state. This led to a mass 'exodus' of Arabs from Palestine, with nearly three-quarters of the Arab population leaving the region. Arab propaganda described them as having been driven out. Jewish propaganda spoke of the Arabs having chosen to leave. What was certain was that a problem had been left that was to curse Middle Eastern politics from that time onwards. Statehood for Israel had created as many problems as it had solved.

Arab–Israeli bitterness

The prospects could not have been worse. Whatever the strength of its claim to separate nationhood, the undeniable truth was that Israel owed its existence at this juncture to terrorism. Between Zionist and Arab nationalist, an unbridgeable gap had been created; idealistic hopes for peace in the area would continue to founder on this intractable hatred. On the day that it came into being, Israel found itself at war with all its Arab neighbours, Syria, Jordan, Iraq and Egypt. Hatred of Israel came to be taken in the Arab world as the chief measure of commitment to Arab nationalism.

The significance of the vendetta did not end there. For centuries the Middle East has been subject to foreign interference. At the end of the First World War, following the collapse of the Ottoman Empire, France and Britain became the chief colonial influences. By 1948 this had largely gone, but outside involvement did not cease. The area now became a theatre for super-power politics. Initially the Soviet Union saw in the new Socialist state of Israel an opportunity to further its interests in a vital area where it had long wished to predominate. Aware of this, the United States was determined not to be put at a disadvantage; the importance of the Middle East as a strategic and oil-producing region was uppermost in American foreign policy considerations. The swift recognition of the state of Israel by both the USSR and the USA were essentially acts of expediency on the part of the great powers bent on maintaining their influence in a key area in international politics. From 1948 the Middle East was a crucible for Zionist aspirations, Arab nationalism and Cold War intrigue.

British colonialism blamed

For many observers, the Middle-Eastern problem was a direct result of colonialism. Certainly the Arab world saw the Suez venture of 1956 (see page 155), involving an Anglo-French-Israeli attack on Egypt, as an attempt to reimpose Western colonialism. Suez illustrated the impossibility of being neutral in the Palestinian question; as far as the Arab-Israeli antagonists were concerned they judged the involvement of outsiders on the principle of 'If you are not for us you are against us.' This had been indicated by the reaction to the formation of the Baghdad Pact in 1955. Signed by Iran, Turkey, Pakistan and Iraq and backed by Britain and the USA, the Pact was intended to provide stability in the Middle East. It had the reverse effect. The Arab states who had not signed up rejected it as neo-colonial and pro-Israeli. Moreover, it provided the Soviet Union with a strong moral justification for involvement in the Middle East since the Pact nations included several Arab states bordering the USSR. The Pact gave cover to the Soviet Union, as a supporter of anti-Zionism, to make overtures to Syria and Egypt and in this way spread its influence in the whole region.

Oil

The question of oil and military strategy was basic to the major powers' interest in the area. Practically unbroken warfare between Israel and the Arab states surrounding her continued through the 1950s and 1960s. Anxieties as to oil and investments lay behind Western attempts to establish stability. The Eastern bloc stood to gain more by instability in the region and this underlay Communist support for Egypt and Syria. Western counter-moves aimed at preserving links with the traditionally pro-Western Arab states while at the same time giving guarantees to Israel.

Israeli development, Arab anger

What deepened the problem was the evident success that Israel made of nationhood. In a remarkably short time, the new Jewish state achieved genuine modernization. Inspired by intense patriotism and greatly aided by financial support from Zionists overseas, Israel soon outstripped her Arab rivals in terms of economic and industrial growth. This superiority was apparent in the military success which Israel achieved continuously in the various wars fought from 1948 onwards. However, Israeli military victory settled nothing. It enabled her to extend her frontiers, but this simply added to her security burdens by stretching her resources and exciting still more Arab bitterness. The plight of dispossessed Arab refugees became a potent emotional and political factor. Notwithstanding her awesome military record, Israel could never, in the nature of the situation, achieve complete security. One major defeat for her was tantamount to national destruction. The Arabs could undergo serious reverse yet still come back to fight another day.

This may partly explain the failure of the Arab states to form a permanent united front. To be anti-Zionist was easy enough; it was far more difficult to agree on much else. Individual state interests often cut across Arab nationalism and weakened effective collective action against the main adversary. But the struggle would continue.

Given Cold War sensitivity, the worldwide dependence on oil, conventional and nuclear strategies, and Arab and Islamic sensibility, the creation of the state of Israel acted as a touch paper to the powder keg. Conceived as a haven for the persecuted, Israel, in Arab eyes, became a symbol of persecution. In this unresolvable dispute in a localized area was added the complexity of super power politics, making the question of Israel and the Middle East an issue of world proportions in the second half of the twentieth century.

The lesson for Britain

The critical lesson for Britain was how powerless it had been in the face of determined Zionism. The abandonment of her mandate showed the limitation of her ability to police international affairs in the post-war world. That lesson was to be brought home even more strongly by the outcome of the Suez venture.

12

the empire in dissolution – Ireland, Suez and Africa

This chapter will cover:
- how independence for Ireland prepared the way for decolonization
- Britain's last imperial venture – the Suez affair
- decolonization in Africa.

A lively debate continues over what was the most critical moment in Britain's abandonment of her empire. Obviously the granting of independence in 1947 to India, 'the jewel in the Crown', was of huge significance. But a quarter of a century earlier, events had taken place in Ireland that might be regarded as of equal importance in Britain's imperial story.

Ireland in colonial history

Ireland is sometimes referred to as Britain's first colonial possession. This is a controversial view, but there are certainly some striking parallels between Britain's relations with Ireland and those with her overseas colonies. Ireland had been under British control, some would say occupation, since the twelfth century. By the nineteenth century a powerful, sometimes violent, Irish nationalist movement was demanding Britain's total withdrawal. The first target was the repeal of the Act of Union of 1801, which, in defiance of the wishes of the majority of the Irish people, had incorporated the island of Ireland into the United Kingdom. Progressive thinkers such as the Liberal leader, Gladstone, came to accept that the union was indefensible and that home rule, Victorian shorthand for independence, must be introduced. Gladstone tried unsuccessfully in 1886 and 1893 to push a Home Rule Bill through parliament. Interestingly, those who opposed home rule did so with similar arguments to those that were to be heard over India. To grant independence would be to strike a fatal blow at 'the integrity of the empire', they said.

Nevertheless, a third Home Rule Bill was eventually passed in 1912. But in some ways this made the position worse. A huge political and practical problem remained. Ireland, which had never been a united nation at any point in its history, contained a significant number of Protestants of the God-fearing and intense Presbyterian variety. These were people, largely of Scottish origin, whose families had been settled in the northern province of Ulster since the seventeenth century. The Ulster Protestants feared that under home rule, they would be swamped and dominated by Catholic southern Ireland. Such were the demands of the Irish nationalists and the fears of the Ulstermen after home rule had been passed that civil war threatened. What prevented this was the outbreak of war in Europe in 1914. It was agreed that the operation of the Home Rule Act would be suspended for the duration of the war.

The Easter Rising, 1916

Suspension of home rule did not solve the Irish problem – it merely shelved it. This became very apparent with the 'Easter Rising' of April 1916 when a breakaway group of the Irish Republican Brotherhood seized the General Post Office in Dublin and proclaimed the establishment of the Irish Republic. After four days of bitter fighting, the republicans were overwhelmed by a British force; their ringleaders were executed after a summary trial. The rising had been poorly supported but the executions turned the rebels into martyrs and intensified Irish bitterness. The Irish poet, W. B. Yeats, spoke of 'a terrible beauty' having been born, a reference to the terrible nature of violence and the uplifting beauty of sacrifice. The British government feared that this Easter Rising might lead to further serious troubles in Ireland. David Lloyd George, a leading member of the War Cabinet, took on the task of finding a solution. His primary concern was to prevent the Irish crisis from undermining the British war effort. He immediately entered into discussions with John Redmond, the Irish Nationalist leader, and Edward Carson, leader of the Ulster Unionists' who were opposed to home rule.

Lloyd George was both a brilliant and an unscrupulous negotiator. He proposed a compromise, referred to as the 'Heads of Agreement'. This granted immediate home rule for the 26 counties of southern Ireland with Ulster remaining part of the United Kingdom until after the war, when its permanent status would be settled. Lloyd George deliberately gave Redmond the impression that the separation of Ulster from the rest of Ireland was purely temporary. At the same time, he reassured Carson that it would be permanent. However, for the moment, Lloyd George's manoeuvring came to nothing. When the Heads of Agreement were put to the Coalition Cabinet the Unionist members refused to ratify it. They claimed Lloyd George had gone too far to appease the Irish nationalists. When Redmond learned of this he broke off negotiations and the Agreement became a dead letter.

Sinn Fein

The failure to achieve a settlement undermined the position of those nationalists in Ireland who believed that a peaceful solution was possible and gave strength to those who argued that force was the only way to get things done. The 80 Irish Nationalist MPs decided that they would no longer attend the Westminster Parliament. Despite this gesture of defiance, the Nationalist Party began to lose ground in Ireland to the more extreme Sinn Fein party (Irish for 'Ourselves Alone'), whose leading members had played a prominent role in the Easter Rising. In 1917, the year in which Eamon de Valera became its leader, Sinn Fein won two by-elections.

The British government made matters worse by trying to extend military conscription into Ireland in 1918. Although Sinn Fein was officially banned, it won 73 seats in the general election held at the end of the war in 1918. Instead of taking these up at Westminster, in 1919 it defiantly set up its own *Dail Eireann* (Irish Parliament) in Dublin. In the same year Sinn Fein's military wing, the Irish Volunteers, reformed itself as the Irish Republican Army (IRA), dedicated to guerrilla war against the British forces. IRA activists became so disruptive that Lloyd George sanctioned the recruitment of special irregular forces to deal with the situation. The most notorious of these were known from the colour of their hastily-designed uniform as the Black and Tans. There were strong rumours that many of them had been recruited from among violent criminals doing time in English gaols. The harsh methods they used soon led to their being hated by Irish nationalists, who accused Lloyd George of employing them deliberately to terrorize the civilian population of Ireland. The Black and Tans became the hated symbols of British authority in Ireland.

The Anglo–Irish Treaty, 1921

Lloyd George, now Prime Minister, claimed publicly 'to have murder by the throat', but the ferocity of the disturbances in Ireland between 1919 and 1921, referred to as 'the troubles', finally convinced him that a settlement acceptable to both Nationalists and Unionists had somehow to be found. So, in 1921, he gathered together a team of negotiators that included the new Conservative leader, Austen Chamberlain as well as Lord Birkenhead, previously one of the staunchest opponents of home rule. He then offered De Valera a truce and invited him and the other Irish leaders to London to discuss the drafting of a treaty of settlement.

When they arrived, Lloyd George shrewdly played upon the idea that he represented the last hope of justice for Ireland. He suggested that if they could not reach an acceptable agreement under his sympathetic leadership he would have to resign and with him would go any chance of a real settlement. His argument persuaded the negotiators to accept the appointment of a boundary commission which would plan how Ulster could be detached from the rest of Ireland. What this acceptance meant was that Irish nationalists had given ground on the critical issue; they had dropped their previous insistence that Ulster must be part of an independent Ireland.

With this as a bargaining factor, Lloyd George was able to convince the Unionists that the rights and independence of Ulster had been safeguarded. In December 1921, after a long and complicated series of discussions in which all Lloyd George's arts of diplomacy and trickery were exercised, the parties finally signed the Irish Treaty, according southern Ireland dominion status as the Irish Free State, with Ulster remaining part of the United Kingdom. This solved the major problem that had afflicted Anglo-Irish relations since the Union of 1801, but it left the Irish Nationalists torn between those who were willing to accept the Treaty, which involved partition and the swearing of an oath of loyalty to the British Crown as the price of freedom, and those, like De Valera, who dismissed the Treaty as a betrayal of Ireland. The tragic result was that between 1922 and 1923 Ireland, in its first years of independence, was blighted by a bitter civil war between the pro-Treaty Nationalists, led by Michael Collins, and the anti-Treaty Republicans led by De Valera.

As immediate and later events in Ireland were to show, the 1921 settlement was far from being a perfect solution. The undeniable fact was that the Treaty was necessarily a compromise, and, as is the way with compromises, it left no one entirely content. The Unionists were left feeling betrayed by Lloyd George's willingness to give in to what they regarded as republican terrorism. For their part, the Nationalists could not regard the Treaty as anything other than a concession reluctantly and belatedly extracted from a British government which granted it only when all other means of maintaining the union had failed. But, above all, it was the partition of Ireland that left the most bitter legacy. It would haunt future generations.

What is fascinating about the Irish settlement is that it established the precedent of withdrawal by Britain when faced by committed, organized, nationalist opposition. It also introduced the notion of partition as a way of settling conflicting nationalist claims. Sadly it also showed that partition is invariably followed by bitterness and bloodshed. The parallel with India in 1947 is a disturbingly exact one.

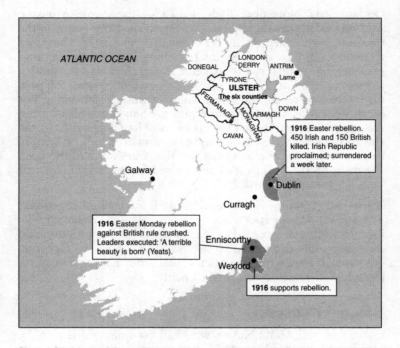

Figure 26 the partition of Ireland, 1921 – map of the 1921 Treaty settlement showing the partition of the island of Ireland into the Irish Free State and Northern Ireland (comprising the six counties). Northern Ireland is sometimes loosely referred to as Ulster, although historically Ulster had been made up of nine counties – the six shown plus Donegal, Cavan, and Monaghan. The fact that Northern Ireland did not include these last three was of immense importance since it left the Protestants in a majority in the north.

The Suez affair, 1956

We saw earlier how Britain had to make a humiliating retreat from Palestine in 1948 when she found she could no longer fulfil her protective role under the UN mandate. Her departure from Palestine and from India a year earlier, revealed how restricted her imperial ambitions had become. In 1956 there occurred a crisis whose outcome convinced many that Britain had ceased to be an imperial power at all.

On an early November night in 1956, the Prime Minister, Anthony Eden was slumped in his seat on the front bench in the Commons chamber. With his sunken eyes, blood-shot and strained from lack of sleep, his trembling hands clenching and unclenching round a sweat-soaked handkerchief, and his sudden jerking upright as his blocked bile duct sent spasms of pain through his stomach, the Prime Minister was a pitiful sight. But on this occasion there was little pity for him, not at least from the opposition who bayed for his blood. Here was a man at the end of his tether. He had aroused the anger of half of Britain, been rejected by the majority of the Commonwealth, been sworn at by the president of the United States, and threatened with a Soviet rocket attack.

What had Anthony Eden done to merit such bitter reactions? The answer was he had tried to impose his will on the Middle East. In what many regard as the last throw of Britain's imperial dice, Eden had attempted to use force to topple the Egyptian government and wrest the Suez Canal from Egyptian control. How had he got into this predicament?

Colonel Nasser

Colonel Gemal Abdul Nasser, who had become President of the new Egyptian republic in 1952, had at first been on good terms with the West. He had been promised American and British loans for the construction of the Aswan Dam, a project on which he had staked his own and his country's future. However, when the USA learned that he had also approached the Soviet bloc countries for aid, it withdrew its original offer. In desperation, Nasser, in July 1956, announced the nationalization of the Suez Canal as a means of raising the necessary finance. Foreign ships would have to pay to pass through what was now an Egyptian waterway.

The British Prime Minister, Anthony Eden, who had come to regard Nasser as an Arab Hitler, declared that such a man could not be allowed 'to leave his thumb on Britain's windpipe', a reference to the threat to the essential oil supplies that came to Britain from the Middle East. He began to plot Nasser's downfall. France, which had long resented Egypt's support for the Arab nationalists in French Algeria, was very willing to join the British against Egypt. Eden also believed that the Americans would give at least diplomatic backing to any Anglo-French attempt to free the Canal. The Americans did, indeed, join Britain and France in trying to apply pressure to Egypt by the creation of a Canal Users' Association. But Nasser refused to budge. Britain and France then referred the issue to the Security Council. However, this proved fruitless, since the Soviet Union vetoed the UN proposals condemning Egypt.

Anglo-French-Israeli collusion

All this confirmed Eden in his belief that only force could shift Nasser. He began secret discussions with the French and the Israelis, who were eager to launch a major strike against Egypt, the chief source of Arab terrorism against them. Plans for a combined military invasion of Egypt were prepared. The strategy, finalized in mid-October 1956, was that the Israelis would attack Egypt across the Sinai peninsula. Britain and France, after allowing sufficient time for the Israelis to reach the Canal, would then mount a joint assault on the Canal region from the north, under the pretence of forcing Egypt and Israel to observe a ceasefire. The plan was accepted by Eden's Cabinet. On 29 October, the Israelis duly attacked across the Gaza Strip; on 30 October the Anglo-French ultimatum was delivered and on the following day the two European allies began their invasion of Egypt. The United Nations entered into an emergency debate in which the Americans, infuriated by Eden's ignoring of them, led the condemnation of Israel and her two allies. President Eisenhower used four-letter words to swear down the phone at Eden. Britain for the first time used its veto in the UN to defeat a resolution demanding an immediate ceasefire. Besides anger, what moved the Americans was their determination not to allow the Soviet Union to seize the initiative.

The USSR entered the dispute dramatically by delivering a diplomatic Note to Britain. Characterizing the Anglo-French invasion of Egypt as the bullying of the weaker by the stronger, the Note contained a thinly-veiled threat that unless Britain withdrew the USSR might consider using rockets against her. It remains unlikely that the USSR would have carried out its threat to attack Britain and British forces directly; it was Britain's temporary international isolation that allowed the Soviet Union

to take a righteous stance and engage in a bluff that it calculated
would not be called. It is true that, the day after the receipt of
the Note, Britain did conform to the UN demand to withdrew
her troops from the Canal zone, but this had little to do with the
Soviet intervention. What led Eden to order the withdrawal
from Egypt was the deep division of opinion at home, as evident
in impassioned parliamentary opposition, the fury of the
Americans and, above all, a run on the pound sterling, which
threatened Britain with economic collapse.

The end of the affair

Eden's career was ended by it all. The strain worsened his
already damaged health. His wife recalled that during the crisis
she felt as if the River Nile was running through her living
room. He resigned the premiership on health grounds, but he
was a broken man politically as well as physically.

Britain's withdrawal from Suez at the point when its forces were
on the verge of military success showed how exposed it felt
diplomatically. Historians view the Suez crisis as a land mark in
Britain's foreign policy. In attacking Egypt, Britain had
attempted to act independently of NATO and the United States,
without consulting the Commonwealth, and in disregard of the
UN. The international and domestic protests that the Suez
venture aroused meant that it was the last occasion Britain
would attempt such unilateral action. Imperialism had made its
last throw. There was a fitting symmetry to this. Britain's
scramble for Africa had begun in Egypt in 1882; her colonial
ambitions ended there 70 years later.

African independence

Whatever the rights and wrongs of Britain's Suez venture, there
is little doubt that the diplomatic reverse she had suffered made
her wary of trying to interfere with the trends and processes of
decolonization that gathered pace in the second half of the
twentieth century. The outstanding example of decolonization
was Africa.

The remarkable transformation that the African continent
experienced in this period can be expressed in simple figures. In
1955 there were five independent states; by 1969 there were 41.
The progress towards decolonization depended for its

smoothness on local circumstances and on whether there was a large or determined white settlement in the area. By the early 1960s, the major colonial powers, France, Britain and Belgium had all accepted the principle of colonial independence. The question now was by what route it would be achieved and what would be the problems for the new African states.

When the British Prime Minister, Harold Macmillan, spoke in South Africa in 1960, of 'the winds of change' blowing through the continent, he was reflecting on the achievement of independence in the former British territories of Ghana, Kenya and Uganda, and warning his white audience that no part of Africa could be isolated from the force of African nationalism. The case of Ghana was particularly significant. The gaining of independence there in 1957 under the leadership of Kwame Nkrumah had set the model for the rest of Africa.

Problems for the new states

While under colonial rule, Africans had been united by their opposition to it; when it ended serious local and tribal rivalries surfaced. Concepts of pan-Africanism, such as those advanced by Nkrumah, were as yet too vague to make real headway. The differences between the states, structured on arbitrary European lines and those based on traditional tribal and ethnic groupings, were a barrier to African federation. There was, furthermore, considerable tension in many areas resulting from conflicting territorial claims. Those states which had powerful personal leaders, like Nkrumah or Sékou Touré of Guinea, often took a strongly national line that did not relate to their neighbours' interests.

These anxieties led in the 1960s to the development of significant groupings. Reaction among Africans to the bloody civil war in the Congo crisis following the Belgian withdrawal and to the Algerian war of independence against France produced two rival blocs, the Union of African States, formed mainly from the ex-French colonies and tending towards political conservatism, and the militant Casablanca Group, made up of Ghana, Guinea, Mali, Morocco and the United Arab Republic, who all avowed socialism as the way ahead for Africa.

The Organization of African Unity

Tensions were eased by the ending of the Algerian war and the overthrow of Patrice Lumumba in the Congo. There was also a shift of interest away from Western and Central Africa to the East where Tanganyika, Uganda and Kenya had recently gained independence. As independence spread across the continent, local boundary issues predominated, lessening the rivalry between versions of African federation. Emperor Haile Selassie acted as mediator, convening an African summit in Addis Ababa in 1963. The outcome was the signing of an African Charter and the creation of the Organization of African Unity. At base, this was an uneasy compromise between moderate leaders concerned for African stability and economic growth, and radicals whose first thought was for ideological struggle and commitment to black revolution in white South Africa.

Cutting across ideas of African unity and common advance was the apparently irresistible tendency for most of the independent states to lapse into despotic, one-party regimes. Nkrumah openly justified 'emergency measures of a totalitarian kind'. Ghana's example was followed elsewhere. Although Nkrumah was deposed in 1966, his overthrow was not the signal for genuine democratic advance in Africa. Parliaments remained frightened servants of the government. In such circumstances opposition could come only from disaffected exiles challenging the regime from abroad and often supported for Cold War reasons by either East or West who dabbled in Africa for political reasons. Civil wars in Nigeria and the Congo were evidence of this.

The concepts that had initially inspired African nationalism, and to which Macmillan had referred, had been self-determination, democracy and constitutionalism. It is, therefore, necessary to explain why, having achieved the first of these aims, the majority of African states did not develop as true democracies. Part of the answer lies in the artificial nature of the states themselves, created according to European ideas of nationhood and not in keeping with ethnic realities. With independence came the re-emergence of tribal differences. In such states as Guinea, Mali, Senegal and Tanganyika, resistance to colonialism had been cross-tribal and local differences had been subordinated to the national struggle. Adoption of a one-party system after independence was logical and largely acceptable. However, in those areas such as the Congo, Dahomey, Nigeria, Kenya and Uganda, where tribal separatism had been pronounced, the party which took over power at the time of independence looked upon opposition to itself as unacceptable. In both types of state, one-party regimes were self-justifying, opposition being dismissed as either unnecessary or treasonable.

The colonial legacy

Another factor was the colonial administrative legacy. During the independence struggles it had been essential for a powerful leader to emerge to unite resistance to the foreigner. With the foreigner gone, this unity broke up and the struggle for succession centred round the control of the administrative system. Centralized and authoritarian by colonial tradition, these systems provided real power to those individuals or groups who could gain effective control of them. In this sense the European empires had laid the base for African political absolutism.

Denied constitutional means, those Africans who sought to challenge the post-independence regimes had to resort to physical methods. As a consequence, control of the military became the key to power in much of Africa. Political instability and chronic economic problems were the justification for a series of military coups. In the early 1960s the governments of Togo, Dahomey and the Congo all fell to military takeover. Less successful challenges occurred in East Africa where the Tanzanian, Ugandan and Kenyan authorities were able to call on British troops for assistance. The French were similarly involved in Gabon in 1964. The UN had earlier been active in the Congo. Direct foreign intervention, however, did not become the order of the day. Coups in Nigeria and Ghana in 1966 were not the result of outside interference. Foreign states were reluctant to become involved unless directly invited by legitimate African governments.

The winds of change

'The winds of change' were essentially the ideals of nationhood and representative government. By the 1960s they had blown down the remnants of colonialism in the whole continent outside white-controlled Southern Africa. But the persistence of political instability, economic weakness, and ethnic regionalism encouraged the growth of undemocratic trends. As the special tragedies of the civil wars in the Congo and Nigeria and the more general difficulties nearly everywhere illustrated, the transition from colonialism to independence would be a time of trauma.

A major problem that confronted Britain in its dealings with the independent African states was what has been described as 'colonial guilt'. In the post-imperial age it was difficult for the ex-colonial powers to criticize the newly-independent states without appearing to be patronizing or neo-colonialist. As Robert Mugabe, the less than democratic leader of Zimbabwe, who came to power after independence in 1980, was fond of saying, 'We need no lectures from our old imperial masters on how to behave.'

13 the people of the empire

This chapter will cover:
- enthusiasm in Britain for the empire
- army life in the empire
- the lives of the expats
- the benefactors.

The size and variety of the British empire means that it is impossible to speak of a typical imperial experience. The empire was a kaleidoscope made of varied people and places. Missionaries, convicts, idealists, adventurers, exploiters, explorers, crooks, pursuers of dreams, escapers from poverty, runners from reality, soldiers who went where they were told not where they chose to go: such were the ordinary and not so ordinary people who helped give the British empire its shape and character. What this chapter does is to look at aspects of the lives of those varied people, whose only common characteristic was that they would not have been where they were or have done what they did had there not been an empire.

Pride and glory

On 22 June 1897, thousands of troops representing every race and land in the empire paraded through London in celebration of Queen Victoria's diamond jubilee. The occasion was both a tribute to her and an expression of the might and extent of the British empire. Victoria's long reign indelibly associated her name with empire; in lauding her the British people were delighting in their imperial strength. During her reign the empire had grown to cover 11 million square miles, a quarter of the globe, and to encompass a quarter of the world's population.

Even more impressive than the sight of the soldiers of the empire marching through London's bedecked and bunting-clad streets filled with cheering millions, was the Spithead naval review. Held four days after the London celebrations, the review was an awesome sight, 'enough', as one newspaper put it, 'to strike terror into the enemy and make the heart of every Briton swell with pride'. Monarchs and ministers of the world, accompanied by the world's press, gathered to watch the splendid affair. It was the greatest ever gathering of ships in one place. The line of vessels stretched for 11 kilometres (seven miles), 170 individual warships dressed overall, their crews totalling in all some 40,000 officers and men, lined up along the rails, nearly all dressed in white.

It was a display of power meant to impress Britain's friends and frighten her foes. Pride and belief in her navy helps to explain why Britain was so disturbed and outraged by Germany's crash programme of warship building in this period. Churchill denounced the German move, remarking 'For Germany, her navy is a luxury; for Britain, it is a necessity.' The mutual suspicion and rivalry that this created was to spill over into war in 1914.

Ordinary people could identify with what Churchill said. They felt threatened by Germany. It is not always easy to distinguish between love of empire and simple patriotism. When the crowds cheered at the relief of Mafeking during the Boer War or joined in the music hall song that gave a new word to the language, jingoism, it is doubtful whether they were aware of any difference: We don't want to fight, but by jingo if we do, we've got the ships, we've got the men, we've got the money too.'

Yet it did not have to be fear. People could simply be stirred by excitement and ceremony. At the coronation celebrations for Elizabeth II in 1953, a young woman heavily pregnant with twins was energetically waving a Union Jack as the contingents of Commonwealth troops proudly marched by. A friendly London policeman remarked that it was a pity the children were just too young to enjoy the occasion. 'Yes', she said, 'but I've taken my knickers off so they can hear the band.'

It was not among the upper ranks of British society but among the working classes that love of empire was at its strongest. This is not surprising when one appreciates that there was scarcely an ordinary family in Britain that did not have relations who had settled overseas, or a close relative – husband, son or brother – in the armed forces that guarded the empire. When working-class people waved national flags and sang rousing music hall ditties about bashing the nation's foes, they did not do so just for fun; they were identifying with their relatives in the far-flung corners of the earth, for it was their people, settlers or soldiers, who had made, or were maintaining, the empire.

This is interestingly captured in some of the street and place names of British cities. To take one example; in the city of Leicester a count of the plaques put up to commemorate important public figures shows that the top five were H. M. Stanley, Queen Victoria, General Gordon, Prince Albert and David Livingstone. Elsewhere some of the poorest regions of Britain's cities rejoiced in such exotic names as Kandahar Street, Lucknow Road, Durban Street, Kimberley Place, Roberts Drive: names that conjured up the people and places of the empire, which the inhabitants or workers knew were important even if they did not always understand why. Every major football league ground has its kop end, a name for the bank behind the goal reminiscent of the hill fought over in the battle at Spion Kop in 1900 during the Boer War.

Life in the army

The British army was the guarantee of the empire's existence, yet its troops did not have the best rewarded or the easiest lives of those who served it. Since they were so poorly paid, the practice had grown up of allowing them to supplement their low income by looting the towns and villages they captured while on campaign. This was sometimes formally condemned by the high command, but more often than not officers chose to ignore the behaviour of their men after a battle. After the siege of the Indian town of Bharatpur in 1826 the troops carried off wagon loads of gold, silver, jewellery, silks and camel-hair shawls. In the hunt for any concealed money or gems, pots were smashed and wooden or earth floors dug up. So frequent was the opportunity for looting that many British officers, and it was the officers who got the first pickings, came to rely upon it as their major source of income. John Malcolm who served in the East India Company army for 20 years amassed some £14,000 in that time, enough, he calculated, together with his £1,500 annual pension to buy his way into the English gentry when he retired.

Soldiers, wives and whores

There was a sharp division between officers and men when it came to the question of wives accompanying the troops when they were sent overseas. Whereas married officers could take their wives with them, the army frowned upon the idea of the ranks marrying at all. Only some 6 per cent of serving soldiers were married. It was felt that single men, undistracted by thoughts of caring for a wife, made better soldiers. That was why the army turned a blind eye to prostitution. Far better for the men to gain their sexual release in a casual, commercial bargain than to become permanently committed. As with naval centres like Portsmouth and Dartmouth, army garrison towns, such as Windsor, Aldershot and Colchester became magnets for prostitutes. Despite local protests at this, little was done at first. Then, when steps were taken at last to control prostitution, it was not for moral reasons, but to check the spread of venereal disease. Parliamentary enquiries revealed that at any one time between a third and a half of the army's rank and file were seriously incapacitated by sexually contracted diseases. The causal link between prostitution and the spread of disease among servicemen became undeniable. A panic reaction followed. Between 1864–9 a series of Contagious Diseases Acts were rushed through parliament. The measures required that in 18 specified towns, women suspected of being prostitutes were to be arrested and made to undergo physical examination.

The enforcement of the Acts led to one of the great public crusades of the Victorian era. Josephine Butler, a formidable upper-class lady, organized a spirited campaign against this brutal victimizing and criminalizing of women. Why, she asked, was a prostitute abused and degraded by the law, while the man who used her services was judged merely to be 'indulging his natural appetites'? Her campaign eventually succeeded; by 1886 the Acts were no longer enforced.

Prostitution and disease did not go away. The comedian Arthur Askey told the story of his being convulsed with suppressed laughter during a Second World War visit by Queen Mary to an army hospital where he was an orderly. In one ward the Queen stopped to make a short speech praising the men for their fortitude in bearing the wounds of war. Nobody dared tell her it was a VD ward for treating soldiers who had picked up gonorrhoea and syphilis.

Churchill the adventurer

Life was tough in the ranks but it could be exciting for an ambitious young officer. Winston Churchill provides an outstanding example of the swashbuckling young man looking for adventure for whom the empire provided the means and the motive. He served as a soldier in India and the Sudan, taking part in the last great cavalry charge of the British army at Omdurman, the battle which crushed the dervishes and left Britain in control of Egypt and the Sudan. But it was as a journalist in the Boer War that he became an international celebrity. He survived a train crash and capture by the Boers before making a daring escape and returning to Britain as a fêted hero. All this made excellent copy for the *Morning Post*, which eagerly published his articles and dispatches from South Africa. He may well have embroidered some of the details but the main parts of his story were as reliable as any of the journalism of the time.

His experiences left him in two minds about the empire's wars. He loved the excitement and the glory but he was also conscious of the waste and futility that so often accompanied the fighting.

After witnessing the slaughter at the Battle of Spion Kop in 1900, he described war as an 'amazing medley of the glorious and the squalid, the pitiful and the sublime'. What his formative foreign travels did make him was an unswerving believer in the British empire. At the age of 16 he had written a poem in praise of the empire, two typical lines of which read: 'God shield our Empire from the might/Of war or famine, plague or blight.'

His service overseas confirmed his belief. Writing to his brother from India in 1897, he spoke of 'this great Empire of ours – to the maintenance of which I shall devote my life'. He was as good as his word, never losing his faith in the British empire as a civilizing force for good. It was why he remained a consistent opponent of Indian independence, claiming – with perfect judgement as events were to prove – that if Britain were to lose India the disintegration of the empire itself would soon follow.

Churchill and the loss of empire

Yet there is a fascinating argument that Churchill more than any other individual, more even than Gandhi or the anti-imperialists, was responsible for the end of the British empire. It is a paradox. Churchill, dedicated upholder of the empire, once said 'I have not become the King's First Minister in order to preside over the liquidation of the British empire.' Yet, runs the argument, he ended up doing precisely that. Resolutely committed to preserving Britain's prestige and power as an imperial nation, he refused to contemplate peace in 1940 at a time when Hitler, who had a great admiration for the British empire, might have been willing to agree to a compromise peace that would have left the empire intact. Instead, Churchill, rejecting any notion of a negotiated settlement with Germany, went on to lead the nation through an exhausting five-year struggle that bankrupted Britain and made her incapable of retaining her overseas territories. By 1945 Britain was so financially and economically drained was that she could carry on into peacetime only by taking huge loans from the USA. The Americans with their strong anti-imperialist tradition were not willing to pay for the upkeep of Britain's empire.

There is neatness and logic to the theory that make it impressive. However, it has the air of being wise after the event. It ignores the atmosphere of 1940 and assumes that Churchill had the option of war or peace genuinely open to him and that Hitler would have kept his word. It also fails to take into account the spirit of the times. The imperial idea, in the sense of a power claiming the right to take territory or to rule people against their will, was dying. It was no longer compatible with the principles of democracy and freedom. This did not mean that imposed rule no longer operated in the world – the Soviet Union and the People's Republic of China after 1949 were examples of controlling powers. But neither of these countries was a democracy. Churchill's old-fashioned brand of imperialism was out of date. It did not need a world war to prove that.

There is also the key consideration that Britain since the Commonwealth Act of 1931 was technically not simply an empire but a Commonwealth. This was more than simply a change of name. It was a recognition that, in future, imperial links would be based on free association not authoritarianism. Perhaps all that can safely be said is that rather than causing the dissolution of the British empire the war had accelerated the process.

The life of the expatriates

From 1815 until the 1930s, some 23 million people emigrated from the UK. The USA was the main attraction, but around 7 million chose the British colonies which offered high wages and cheap land.

Many colonists came to inhabit a distorted, even an unreal, world. The expats who lived comfortable lives in parts of the far-flung empire, such as Kenya, Rhodesia or India, waited on by bearers and servants, were only at a level of income that back home in Britain would not have afforded them this elevated style of living. They were exploiting the relative poverty of the regions they had settled in. It was a powerful motive for their wanting to cling onto the privileges that went with colonization.

Boredom could set in and produce odd behaviour. One English diarist recorded in the 1840s how manners had declined among the Europeans while he had been in India. Whereas polite drinking of toasts had been the norm, it had now become a regular practice at gatherings to drink too much and engage in food fights. Cheered on by the ladies, the men would pelt each other with chicken carcasses. Then the ladies would join in the fun by throwing cakes and pastries. 'This', the diarist observed 'was thought wit in refinement and breeding.'

The wealthier expatriates tended to congregate together as an exclusive group. They took their pleasures together: polo, horse racing, big-game hunting and even foxhunting with the riders dressed in the outfits they wore in the English shires. As is so often the case with people who settle or live for long periods away from their own country, they tended to become very patriotic, idealizing the land they had left and attempting to recreate its customs and values in their new home.

The country club became the centre of social life, with the men drinking and gambling or playing billiards in their special lounges and the women playing endless rubbers of bridge and indulging in the gossip which flourishes in such confined communities. Balls and fancy dress soirées, croquet and tennis parties, and amateur dramatics filled out the days and nights and provided the occasions for the scandals on which the gossip fed.

The British Raj did not regard Indians as equals. An unofficial apartheid developed. Save as waiters and orderlies, Indians were not allowed in the British clubs. Discrimination was often as much a matter of class as of race. The British lower ranks were not allowed in the officers mess and the wives of officers and high ranking officials did not mix with the womenfolk of humble British clerks or workers. British officials were unwilling to mix with their own lower orders but they saw no difficulty in consorting with princes, rajahs and their high officials.

The Indian people had their own class, or caste, system. Based on the Hindu religious belief in reincarnation, there was a hierarchy stretching down from the Brahmins at the top to the untouchables who were good only for the most servile and degrading work. There is a suggestion that the British deliberately emphasized and encouraged the caste system since it made British rule easier to operate.

There were exceptions to this of course. Some Britons developed a genuine interest in the cultures, languages, history and archaeology of India. As elsewhere in the empire, some even chose to 'go native', a reference to Europeans adopting the dress and manners of the locals and perhaps going off to live with them. The term also covered eccentric behaviour that might now be diagnosed as a form of mental breakdown. Unable to cope with the climate or the strangeness of foreign parts, some expatriates threw up their jobs and responsibilities and 'went native'.

There were complaints that the bringing of wives to India and other parts of the empire had a bad influence on the husbands since they tended to put domestic concerns before their work. But single men also presented a problem. Alone in a foreign country they were very likely to strike up liaisons with local women. The British authorities or employers usually turned a blind eye to this provided scandal was avoided. But embarrassments could arise when officials who had been used to comforting themselves with local women then brought their wives to the colony. The story is told of a district commissioner who married in England and brought his bride to his base in Nigeria for their honeymoon. At four in the morning of their first night together, the commissioner's servant walked into the bedroom, woke the bride with a firm smack on her bottom, and said, 'Missy, you leave now, time you go back to your village.'

Problems could arise over the children of European-Indian sexual liaisons. Half-castes often went unacknowledged by their British fathers, and the mothers could find themselves and their children unacceptable in their own villages. In the worst cases, such children became rejected, feral scavengers whose only salvation might be one of the orphanages set up by the Christian missionaries. Here was a case of Europeans cleaning up a mess of their own making.

Such cases may give one too jaundiced a view of the expatriates. It must not be forgotten that many, if not most, of the British were dedicated workers. Colonial governments built hospitals, universities and libraries, where local people were trained in Western ways – law, medicine, science and the arts. British women played a leading role in all this. Colonial officers' wives played a major part in establishing hospitals and training nurses. Projects such as how to prevent baby and infant deaths became a special concern.

Tales from the Raj

The story of the end of the British Raj is often written as a grand historical sweep, involving the dramatic decision to bring the date forward, the bitter compromise over partition, the violent Hindu-Muslim-Sikh cross-migrations of millions of people that came after. It is perfectly fitting that it should be described in this way for that was how it happened. But it is also vital to consider how these great events impacted upon ordinary individuals who played no part in bringing them about but whose lives were fundamentally changed by them. Three examples invite attention.

The servant

Chandra had served in the house of the Colonel Bellamy in Bombay. For nearly 30 years he had been the dignified, uncomplaining presence in the house. As butler-cum-chief-steward he provided reliability and stability. He directed the other servants, organized the meals and the many chores and duties attached to the running of a large house. He presided over the grand dinners that the Colonel and Mrs Bellamy hosted. Chandra had no other life. He was always there, at whatever time of day or night the family needed him. He never seemed to sleep. Close as he physically was to the Bellamys and their children as they grew up, the family never really knew how he felt about them, only that he served them with total commitment for over 30 years. He kept his own counsel. He seemed to be thinking deep thoughts but there was no way of knowing whether this was so. His views of the British, of his countrymen, of the politics of India remained a closed book. When the time came for the Bellamys to leave India, he displayed the same measured efficiency in arranging the details of their departure. At the final farewell, he wished the family good fortune, and nodded deferentially when the Colonel praised him for the honest and dutiful man he was. But whether Chandra was pleased or saddened by their going, whether he delighted in the new-won independence of his country, or whether he looked with trepidation to the future, he gave no sign. Independence did not treat him kindly. After the British had left, he found it difficult to find work. His long attachment to the Raj earned him the scorn of some of his fellow Indians. Eventually he became a commissionaire in a New Delhi international hotel. Chandra still retained his great sense of dignity, but although he never said so, it may be that he was not entirely happy in the new India.

The family

The liner *Strathmore* bound from Bombay for Tilbury contained many English families. One of them, the Burns Sweeney family, knew nothing of the Britain they were bound for. The father, 44-year-old Donald, the grandson of a soldier who had fought in the Indian mutiny, and Catherine May, the 34-year-old mother, were of Scottish-Irish stock, but they had lived their whole lives in India. They and the nine surviving of their ten children – six girls, Diana (16), Beulah (15), Vivian (13), Betty (8), six-month-old twins, Agnes and Rose Eleanor, and three boys John (10), Paul (6) and Geoffrey (4) – had known no other land.

Donald who had been educated in Calcutta at a college run by an Irish order of Christian brothers, had been manager of a large railway marshalling yard in Bihar. He and his family had lived well. Servants had relieved his wife of many of the burdens of motherhood. Ayahs tended to the younger children while the older ones went off to boarding school for nine months of the year. Catherine May later joked that she was never quite sure how many children she had until she counted them all when the girls came home for the holidays. The girls added that every time they came home there was a new baby. Their servants wept when the time came, as for so many expat British families, to leave India in a rush after independence.

The Burns Sweeneys came to a gray world of overcast skies. Britain in 1948 was at one of its low points. Shortages and rationing were features of the austerity programme adopted to see through Britain's post-war economic crisis. Six months after arriving in England, the father died. The medical certificate recorded the cause of death as thrombosis. The truth was he died of a broken heart. Struggling to find a job that matched his talents intensified the burden and worry of bringing up a large family in an unfamiliar land. He missed the colour, the smell, the taste, the light and heat of India.

Catherine May now widowed at 35 with nine dependent children, the oldest of whom was 17, the youngest one year, had to make an extraordinary feat of adjustment. Rags to riches is a fairly easy journey; riches to rags, the path she had to take, is altogether different. But she made it. She worked, she skivvied, she scrimped, she saved. The family lived in cramped, shared accommodation but they came through. As the oldest son said at her funeral in 2000: 'she clothed us, she fed us, she gave us love.' It is not a dramatic story, but rather one of quiet heroism. Of such detail was the tapestry of the British empire woven.

The club owner

Not all the British left after independence. A few chose to stay and take their chance in the new India. One such was Bob Wright. He said he loved India too much to leave, come what may. To the amused delight of the Indians, he entered a time warp. For half a century after independence he managed the Tollygunge social club in Calcutta, preserving the style and manners of the old Raj. Brown Windsor soup and lamb chops was always on the members' menu and pink gins were always available in the bar. But it was not simply a study in nostalgia.

Wright became a great organizer of charities concerned with the welfare of orphaned children and the elderly. Mother Teresa, the inspirational Albanian nun, who created the havens for the destitute and the dying in India's cities, annually sent train and tram loads of children to be entertained at the 'Tolly jolly days' that Wright laid on in the extensive gardens and grounds of his club. It was those grounds that he turned into a menagerie and conservation park, frightening off poachers with rifle shots. He worked with the Indian authorities to preserve the tiger, the rhino and the elephant.

The club became caught up in the political difficulties that beset India in the 1970s. One of the club's officials was murdered in an attack by the Naxalites, a Maoist terrorist group. But he and his wife, Ann, were not to be deterred. They continued enthusiastically with their charitable and conservation work until he died, aged 80, in his apartment at the Tollygunge club in the spring of 2005. He had a grand and fitting send off. So many thousands filled the streets to pay their respects that they caused a traffic jam that was monumental even by Calcutta's gargantuan standards. His ashes were scattered in the club grounds. A local Calcutta paper commented. 'Now that he can give no more to India, the soil of India gives him permanent rest.'

The Shanghai sailors of Liverpool

The soldiers and sailors of the empire who fought for Britain during the Second World War made an indispensable contribution. Sadly their post-war fate was not always in keeping with the sacrifice they had made. One notorious case concerned the so-called 'Shanghai sailors'. These were Chinese seamen recruited in Shanghai to serve in the British merchant fleet. Many of them crewed the ships that made the perilous crossings which helped sustain Britain during the Battle of the Atlantic. Their main port was Liverpool and it was in the docklands area there that most of them stayed between sailings. By the end of the war a number of them had married local women and were living in the cheap accommodation that they had rented or bought. When the war ended they hoped to stay in Britain. But in an extraordinary act of ingratitude the government decreed that they were to be repatriated. In June 1946, Liverpool's China town witnessed distressing scenes as over the course of two days some 2,000 Chinese seamen were rounded up in vans and taken to the docks where they were forcibly put aboard waiting ships. It was a carefully planned operation directed by the police Special Branch, in co-operation with Liverpool Council, acting on Home Office orders.

The reasons given for the repatriation included: the need for housing to be made available to local people, and to stamp out the vices associated with the seamen, namely; opium smoking, gambling and the spread of venereal disease. These claims were blatantly false. The houses from which the Chinese were evicted had in many cases been earlier bought by them in cash and so were their legitimate property. There was also a law which stated that foreigners whose spouses were British were entitled to stay in Britain. The authorities got round this simply by saying that the women whom the men had married were really only prostitutes and that the marriages did not, therefore, qualify. As to the charge of opium use, the bitter irony was that the Britain which was now expelling the seamen was the same nation that had forced the drug upon the Chinese 100 years earlier. The women whose husbands were snatched from them, and the children who lost their fathers, were never given any compensation or even an explanation. The whole episode was a form of ethnic cleansing.

Small deeds, big effects

But the record of empire is not all gloom. The list of benefactors who quietly got on with things and produced often extraordinary results is uplifting. There was Ronald Ross, the Indian army surgeon who in 1897 discovered that malaria was spread by mosquito bites. His researches saved millions of lives the world over. Less publicized, but in its own way a contribution to human good, was the technique developed by the Reverend Jay Lennard. As a district commissioner in Ghana in the years 1924–52, he was responsible for settling land and property disputes. Not always able to grasp a particular dialect he had to rely on interpreters. He got to know purely from the way the witness, the translator or the court laughed whether he was being told the truth.

The words of Philip Bowcock, a district officer in one of the remoter areas of the Sudan where he worked among the Dinka people, are worth quoting as a corrective to the idea that corruption was the norm among administrators. 'My memory is of laughter. The officers were invariably decent and honest men.

No people ever feathered their nest less than the British in my area.'

Robert Bruce is a name that conjures up the Anglo-Scottish rivalry of medieval times. But in addition to the Scottish king, there was another Robert Bruce who was equally important in his own way. It was Major Robert Bruce who in 1823 discovered that tea grew in abundance in the forests of Assam, a north-eastern province of India. Over a generation he created the great tea gardens that produced the crop of black tea that Britain eagerly devoured. Black tea is the fermented form of the green leaf variety. The making of a proper cup of tea is one of Britain's great historical accomplishments. It is an art that no other country has ever succeeded in matching.

14 the end of the empire

This chapter will cover:
- the military legacy of empire
- the strain of war
- British engagements after 1945
- empire in reverse – Commonwealth immigration into Britain.

The empire at war

The empire had not been created to fight wars, but when war came it proved very useful. Without the dominions and colonies to call on, Britain could not have won either of the two world wars. This is evident in the scale of the military contribution the empire made.

	Total troops	Killed	Wounded
UK	5,700,000	702,000	1,670,000
India	1,400,000	64,000	167,000
Canada	630,000	56,700	150,000
Australia	420,000	59,300	152,000
South Africa	136,000	7,000	12,000
New Zealand	129,000	16,000	41,300

Total number of troops and casualty figures, 1914–18

To these figures could be added over 1 million non-combatants from the empire who served as porters and labourers in the various war fronts in Europe and Africa. In 1918 there were over 300,000 workers from North Africa and China behind the lines on the western front.

	Total troops	Killed and missing	Wounded
UK	4,650,000	290,513	275,975
India	1,789,000	35,559	62,064
Canada	770,000	38,884	53,073
Australia	579,000	27,934	37,477
New Zealand	97,000	12,045	19,253
South Africa	150,000	8,397	13,773
African colonies	421,000	21,552	60,773

Total number of troops and casualty figures, 1939–45

The impact of war on the empire

Britain was an eventual winner in both world wars. Yet by another irony the wars hastened the empire towards its eventual disintegration for they exposed Britain's economic weakness and encouraged challenges to her authority. This was very evident in the early years of the Second World War in the Far East. On Christmas day, only two weeks after the start of the Pacific War, Hong Kong was captured by the Japanese. Two months later on 15 February 1942, Singapore, Britain's main naval base, fell to Japan. This was largely the result of a brilliant rapid march down the Malay peninsula by Japanese forces who then took the base from the undefended north. All the defenders' guns were facing south out to sea expecting a naval attack. Some 70,000 British and Commonwealth troops surrendered and were taken into what was to be a long and brutal captivity. The fall of Singapore was described by Churchill as 'the worst disaster and largest capitulation in British history'. There followed a string of Japanese victories in south-east Asia. It would take over three years of desperate, dedicated and courageous fighting for the Allies to regain what had been lost. When that was achieved, British colonial administration was reimposed on all the recovered territories.

But it was all rather hollow. The war had worked a fundamental change. There would be no return to the status quo. Despite the heroism of the British and imperial troops, in particular the tenacity of the Australian and New Zealand contingents, the invincibility of British armies had been shown to be a myth. The initial defeats inflicted by the Japanese had left the vulnerability of Britain's empire glaringly exposed. Notions of white superiority might linger on for a while but they became increasingly difficult to believe or justify.

Major British military engagements, 1948–99

Britain's imperial legacy is nowhere more clearly shown than in the military conflicts into which it was drawn in the half century that followed the end of the Second World War. It was a bitter paradox that after ceasing to be an empire Britain should have been so involved in struggles whose long-term origins lay in its imperial history.

The Malayan Emergency, 1948–66

The Malay peninsula, rich in tin and rubber and of vital strategic importance, contained nine independent states under British protection and three British settlements including Singapore. On 1 February 1948, these states formally came together as the Federation of Malaya. Although the area was multi-racial, the two largest groups were native Malays and expatriate Chinese. Backed by Mao Zedong's People's Republic of China, the Malay Chinese began a Communist guerilla insurrection against the Federation. Responding to an appeal from the Malay government, Britain sent forces to the area, declared an emergency, and began a series of determined anti-Communist campaigns, joined by troops from a range of Commonwealth countries.

After six years of fierce fighting the Communist insurgents finally withdrew from Malaya in 1954. Britain signed a defence and mutual assistance with Malaysia in 1957. This was put to the test in 1963 when President Sukarno of neighbouring Indonesia declared the Federation of Malaysia was 'neo-colonialist' and ordered Indonesian raids on the area. In defending Malaysia, British and Commonwealth forces suffered over 300 casualties before a peace settlement was signed in Bangkok in June 1966.

The Cyprus Emergency, 1952–9

Since the late nineteenth century Britain had maintained a presence in the strategically valuable island of Cyprus in the eastern Mediterranean. Eighty per cent of the island's population were of Greek origin; the other 20 per cent were Turkish. The Greek majority demanded the union of Cyprus with Greece (*enosis*). When Britain declined to grant this, EOKA, the militant wing of the *enosis* movement turned to terrorism against British forces and the Turkish minority. A complex and bloody civil war followed before a ceasefire was agreed in March 1959, followed a year later by the creation of the Independent Republic of Cyprus. However, the bitterness between Greeks and Turks remained and an uneasy truce was kept only by partitioning the island.

The Kenyan Emergency, 1952–60

In an effort to preserve stability in the East African colonies of Tanganyika, Uganda and Kenya, Britain proposed that these areas form an East African Federation. The official line was that the Federation would pursue multi-racial, equal shares policies. However, in Kenya where white settlers dominated the government and owned the best land it was unlikely that genuine social or political equality would follow. The Kikuyu, Kenya's largest native tribe, began to organize resistance. This took its most violent form in the shape of the Mau Mau secret society. Between 1952 and 1959 thousands of British troops were deployed in Kenya. A grim cycle of Mau Mau outrages and British coercion occurred before the state of emergency was ended in 1960. It is a deeply unpleasant story. Recent research suggests that the British forces imposed a reign of terror. The casualty figures are very revealing. Around 100 Europeans and 13,000 native Kenyans lost their lives in the violence.

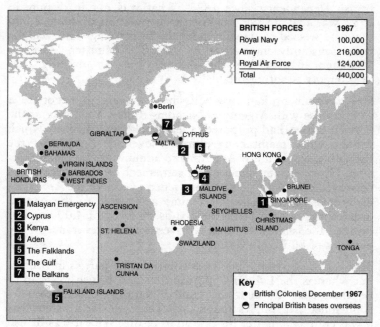

Figure 27 the main British military engagements after 1945

Aden, 1963–7

Aden, a key strategic port at the southern end of the Red Sea had been a British protectorate since the early nineteenth century. In the post-war world, Arab nationalists began to demand independence for Aden. In 1963 Britain faced increasing internal unrest and cross-border attacks from Yemen. Following a four-year conflict during which 50 British troops were killed and 650 wounded, Britain withdrew after recognizing Aden independence within the People's Republic of South Yemen.

The Falklands War, 1982

The legal ownership of the Falklands Islands in the south Atlantic had long been disputed between Argentina and Britain. The historical arguments over sovereignty were complicated. Britain's position was that the Falklands had legally been a British Dependency since 1833. What was not in dispute in 1982 was that 98 per cent of the population of some 2,000 islanders wished to remain under the British flag. This was the point constantly emphasized by the Prime Minister, Margaret Thatcher. It gave her the justification for insisting that 'sovereignty is not negotiable'.

Her government had originally been willing to negotiate a compromise with Argentina. Nicholas Ridley, a minister at the Foreign Office, had proposed 'a leaseback' agreement by which Britain, while maintaining ultimate sovereign rights over the Falklands, would allow Argentina to administer the region as its own. However, any chance of a settlement on these terms was destroyed on 2 April 1982 when General Galtieri, the Argentine dictator, eager to make his regime acceptable to the nation, ordered the seizure of the Falklands. A force of 4,000 troops invaded the islands and quickly overcame the resistance of the garrison of 80 Royal Marines.

This act of aggression was condemned by all parties in Britain, but whereas the Labour opposition wanted British reaction to be channelled through the United Nations, which formally condemned Argentina's action, Mrs Thatcher was insistent that it was entirely a matter for Britain to resolve since it was British sovereignty that had been affronted and British people put under occupation. Mrs Thatcher immediately ordered the retaking of the Falklands. A British Task Force was rapidly put together and sailed from Portsmouth and Southampton. On

25 April, South Georgia, which Argentina had also seized, was recaptured. Air strikes began on 1 May against the occupying Argentine forces on the Falklands.

On 2 May, having placed a 200-mile exclusion zone around the islands, Britain began its naval campaign. In an action that caused controversy in Britain, a British submarine sunk the Argentine cruiser *Belgrano* when it was heading out of the exclusion zone. Two days later HMS *Sheffield* was destroyed by an Argentine Exocet missile. In subsequent engagements two British frigates were also sunk and others damaged in air attacks. However, the Royal Navy had prepared the way effectively for British troop landings to begin on 21 May. By the end of the month the two key areas of San Carlos and Goose Green had been recaptured. The climax came with the liberation of Port Stanley on 14 June. Argentina then surrendered. The conflict had claimed the lives of 255 British and 665 Argentine servicemen. Though some found it tastelessly jingoistic, Mrs Thatcher's cry of 'rejoice, rejoice' at the news of the Task Force's victory found an echo with the population at large who read the tabloid press. People likened her to Churchill in her ability to inspire the nation in wartime.

Having regained the Falklands through battle, Mrs Thatcher let it be known she had no intention of negotiating them away. A large permanent British garrison was to be established on the islands to guarantee their security. When it was suggested they might be put under a UN trusteeship, the Prime Minister rejected the notion with what might be regarded as perhaps the last great expression of the imperial spirit. In words that recalled Pitt, Palmerston and Churchill, she declared: 'Our men did not risk their lives for a UN trusteeship. They risked their lives for the British way of life, to defend British sovereignty. I do not intend to negotiate on the sovereignty of the islands in any way except for the people who live here.'

The Gulf War, 1991

Following the occupation in 1990 of Kuwait by its Arab neighbour, Iraq, a former British protectorate, the United Nations condemned the invasion as an act of aggression. Acting in accordance with a UN resolution, the USA, Britain, and a number of Arab states, formed a military alliance and called upon Saddam Hussein, the Iraqi leader, to withdraw his troops. When he refused Britain joined the USA in dispatching land and naval forces to the Gulf region. After months of preparation an attack was finally launched by the Allies. This proved successful in its immediate aim; Kuwait was liberated and Iraq was required to dismantle much of its weaponry. Saddam Hussein, however, remained in power in Iraq. His refusal to co-operate with UN inspection teams and his acts of genocide against the Kurds within Iraq led the UN to impose economic sanctions which caused considerable distress to ordinary Iraqis. But it required another controversial war in 2004 before Saddam Hussein was finally overthrown.

The empire dismantled

The granting of Indian independence in 1947 had first opened the way for the break up of the whole British empire. Some protests were heard among the British people but these were made from a sense of nostalgia rather than any real belief that empire could be justified and preserved in the modern age. There was a general acceptance that decolonization was essential in a time of democracy and representative government. Between 1957 and 1968 Britain gave independence to all its remaining colonies in Africa and the majority of those elsewhere. For the most part this proved a remarkably smooth and bloodless process. Britain did not experience the bitter colonial wars that France underwent in trying to cling on to its empire. Where there were problems in the British retreat they arose not over whether independence was to be granted but when. However, there was one major exception – Southern Rhodesia.

The Rhodesian Unilateral Declaration of Independence (UDI), 1965–80

The white settler community, which held the political power in Rhodesia, refused to accept the principles of 'majority rule' and 'one person, one vote'. They claimed that majority rule in Rhodesia would give authority to the backward black Africans, who were incapable of exercising it responsibly. Having failed to reach agreement with successive British governments, Ian Smith, the Prime Minister and leader of the white Rhodesian Front Party, declared UDI in1965. For the next 15 years Rhodesia defied international condemnation. But eventually a combination of economic sanctions and a dispiriting civil war forced Smith to the conference table. Talks with Margaret Thatcher's Conservative government produced a new settlement which accepted majority rule. Free elections in 1980 saw a victory for Robert Mugabe, who had been a black guerrilla fighter against UDI. The new nation adopted the name Zimbabwe. The main problem that remained after independence was how long the majority of black Zimbabweans would continue to tolerate the possession of the nation's best land by the minority white farmers. By the beginning of the twenty-first century land confiscation had become an official and brutally enforced policy. It was an act of revenge that was as understandable as it was objectionable. But by this time blacks as well as white Zimbabweans had begun to suffer under a regime that had descended into tyranny.

An idea of both the extraordinary size of the British empire and the equally extraordinary speed with which it was dismantled can be gained from the list on page 187.

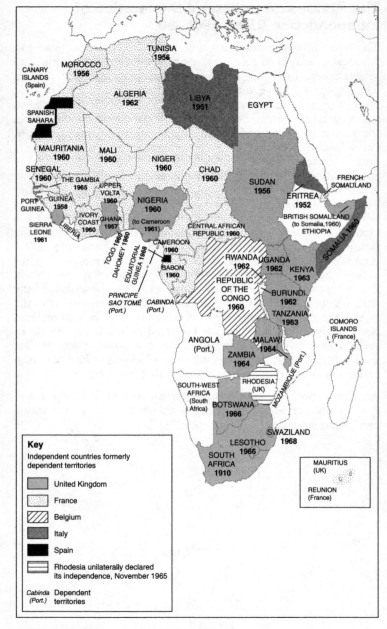

Figure 28 the decolonisation of Africa, 1956–68

Dates of colonies gaining independence (new name in brackets)

1947 – India, Pakistan
1948 – Burma (Myanmar)
1956 – Sudan
1957 – Gold Coast (Ghana), Malaya
1960 – Nigeria, Somalia, Cyprus
1961 – Sierra Leone, Tanganyika and Zanzibar (Tanzania), Kuwait
1962 – Uganda, Jamaica, Trinidad and Tobago
1963 – Kenya, Seychelles; Malaya, Singapore, North Borneo and Sarawak formed Malaysia
1964 – Northern Rhodesia (Zambia), Nyasaland (Malawi), Malta
1965 – Singapore, Gambia, Maldives
1966 – Basutoland (Lesotho), Bechuanaland (Botswana), Barbados, British Guiana (Guyana)
1968 – Swaziland, Mauritius
1970 – Fiji, Tonga
1971 – Bahrain, Qatar, Trucial Oman (United Arab Emirates)
1972 – Ceylon (Sri Lanka)
1973 – Bahamas
1974 – Grenada
1978 – Dominica, Ellice Island (Tuvalu)
1979 – Gilbert Islands (Kiribati), St Lucia, St Vincent and the Grenadines
1980 – Southern Rhodesia (Zimbabwe), New Hebrides (Vanatu)
1981 – British Honduras (Belize)
1983 – Brunei, St Christopher and Nevis
1997 – Hong Kong

In 2005 all that was left of the British empire were the following:

- Anguilla
- Bermuda
- British Antarctica Territory
- British Indian Ocean Territory
- British Virgin Islands
- The Cayman Islands
- The Falkland Islands

- Gibraltar
- Montserrat
- Pitcairn
- South Georgia and South Sandwich Islands
- St Helena
- The Turks and Caicos Islands.

Immigration

A remarkable consequence of the end of empire was that many of the people of the colonies and dominions, who had always been encouraged to look upon Britain as the mother country, came to the United Kingdon to settle. It might be described as a reverse migration, contrasting with the movement the other way in the days of empire when settlers had gone from Britain to the colonies. It explains one of the most notable features of Britain in the second half of the twentieth century – its development as a multi-racial society.

The *Empire Windrush*

The story may be said to begin in 1948 with the sailing of a converted troopship, *Empire Windrush*, from Kingston, Jamaica, to Britain. The ship carried hundreds of Jamaican workers; the majority were young males but there were also a number of older men and families. They were coming to find work. The official welcome they received was a warm one. Cinema newsreels enthusiastically recorded the event and assured the newcomers that they would soon find homes and jobs. Under existing law, the newcomers had full rights of British citizenship. This encouraged further emigration from the West Indies. The government encouraged this with organized appeals for Caribbean workers to fill the vacancies, principally in the hospital and transport services, that Britain's acute post-war labour shortage had left. By the mid-1950s employers in Britain has extended their recruitment to the Indian sub-continent. Textile firms in London and the north of England eagerly took on workers from India and Pakistan.

However, by the late 1950s, disturbing reactions had begun to occur among some of the white population. 'No coloured' notices appeared in boarding house windows and on factory gates. Mutterings were heard to the effect that the newcomers were attracted to Britain as much by the generous welfare benefits as by the prospect of work. The actual number of white residents who believed such slanders may have been small but troublemakers were able to exploit the housing shortage that was a major problem in the poorer areas by suggesting that it was all the fault of the immigrants.

Decade	Outflow	Inflow
1900–09	4,404,000	2,287,000
1910–19	3,526,000	2,224,000
1920–9	3,960,000	2,590,000
1930–9	2,273,000	2,361,000
1940–9	590,000	240,000
1950–9	1,327,000	676,000
1960–9	1,916,000	1,243,000
1970–9	2,554,000	1,900,000
1980–9	1,824,000	1,848,000

migration to and emigration from the UK (to nearest 100,000)

	Old Commonwealth	New Commonwealth	Total
1961	307,697	289,058	596,755
1971	528,810	765,095	1,293,905
1981	350,382	915,768	1,266,150
1991	905,960	1,729,451	2,635,411

Commonwealth immigrants living in the UK

The New Commonwealth comprised largely West Indians, Indians, Pakistanis and Bangladeshis. The Old Commonwealth comprised Australians, New Zealanders, Canadians, and South Africans.

Race relations problems have never been simply about numbers. Extremists who spoke of Britain being 'swamped' by 'waves of immigrants' were talking nonsense. The proportion of people of non-European origins has never been more than 6 per cent of the overall population of Britain. Moreover, as the table shows, in every decade of the twentieth century net emigration exceeded net immigration. The main difficulties arose over accommodation. Immigrants tended, quite naturally given their limited resources when they first arrived in Britain, to live in the poorer areas of cities and urban areas. This was where cheaper properties for buying or renting were. But since Britain suffered from a severe shortage of reasonably-priced housing there was bound to be competition between residents and newcomers.

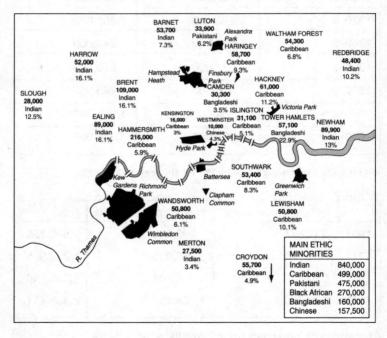

Figure 29 numbers and concentration of ethnic minorities in London in 1991

Social tensions

The tension that immigration caused was evident in the rioting that broke out in 1958 in Nottingham and Notting Hill in London. Long prison sentences were imposed on the white ringleaders of the disturbances but the authorities interpreted the disorder as indicating the need to control the number of New Commonwealth immigrants. A Commonwealth Immigrants Act was introduced in 1962. This was highly controversial and condemned in many quarters as being racist since it placed restrictions on would-be entrants according to their ethnic origin. A second Commonwealth Immigrants Act in 1968 attempted to limit immigration by creating a voucher scheme which restricted the right of entry to those who actually had jobs lined up for them. To show that immigration policy was not based on race prejudice, Race Relations Acts were introduced in 1965, 1968 and 1976; these outlawed racial discrimination in employment, education and training, and in the provision of goods and services, and made it an offence to provoke racial hatred. A Commission for Racial Equality (CRE) was set up to monitor the workings of the Acts.

One consequence of the first Immigration Act in 1962 was a rush of immigrants into Britain in the period before its terms came into force. Between 1960 and 1962, over 230,000 New Commonwealth citizens entered. This in fact marked an immigration peak but the numbers fuelled the anxieties of those who called for a complete block on entry. Voice was given to these concerns by Enoch Powell, an intellectually gifted but maverick Conservative politician, who was Minister of Health from 1960 to 1963. Ironically, during this time he had actively encouraged the recruitment of Commonwealth immigrants as nurses and hospital workers.

An intense nationalist, with a frightening gaze, Powell regarded unlimited immigration as a threat to the character of the UK. In a notorious speech in 1968 he gave his nightmare vision of a future Britain torn by racial conflict. Quoting Virgil's *Aeneid*, he prophesied: 'As I look ahead, I am filled with foreboding. Like the Roman, I seem to see "the River Tiber foaming with much blood"'. The speech was condemned from all sides and effectively ended his career in top level politics. Significantly, Powell remained the only politician of note who took an openly racist stance on immigration.

The immigration and race relations measures were undeniably well intentioned but they had limited success in improving racial harmony. Again the economic situation contributed largely to this. It was one thing to introduce laws against discrimination, it was another to enforce them. The inflation that followed the oil-price crisis of the early 1970s appeared to have the worst effects in immigrant areas where there were disproportionately higher numbers of unemployed than in the population at large. The frustration of the immigrant community, particularly of second and third generation West Indians who had been born and brought up in Britain, was expressed in serious riots in 1981 in Brixton, Birmingham, Bristol and Liverpool and tragically in 1985 when a policeman was killed during the Tottenham Broadwater Farm riot.

'Institutional racism'

The feeling among the black community that they were subject to unwarranted harassment by the police was a continuous grievance. The killing in South London of Stephen Lawrence, a black teenager, by a gang of white youths, who went unconvicted, led eventually to a commission of enquiry which, in its 1999 report, accused the Metropolitan Police of being 'institututionally racist'. This did not seem to augur well for the future of race relations in the new millennium. Yet it would be wrong to end on a depressing note. Much had been achieved in terms of broad shifts of attitude. By 2000, the young of all races in Britain seemed far less worried about racial differences and much more willing to mix socially than their parents and grandparents had been. In that year, the Chairman of the CRE, Trevor Philips, a black writer born in Britain of Guyanan parents, wrote enthusiastically of what had happened in his own city of London. 'London is on the verge of doing what every great world city has tried in vain – to welcome all comers and embrace them with ease and comfort.'

15

the British empire in retrospect

This chapter will cover:
- the character of the British empire
- the debate over the pros and cons of British imperialism
- economic factors
- the record of the empire.

The character of the British empire

It would be more accurate to describe the British empire as the Celtic empire since in its early stages it was explored and settled overwhelmingly by Scotsmen and Irishmen. In the eighteenth century the Scots made up only 10 per cent of the population of Britain yet they provided nearly 60 per cent of those Britons who settled overseas. To take two examples: of the 254 doctors recruited by the East India Company, 132 were Scots. At any one time during the empire's history, two thirds of the rank and file of the army were Irish.

There have been over 60 empires in recorded history, but there never has been one quite like Britain's. At its greatest extent it covered one quarter of the globe and contained one sixth of the world's population. It spread across so many continents that it was literally true that the sun never set on the empire; there was always some British colony or possession where it was daytime. Yet it had never been planned to be so vast. In fact, it had not really been planned at all. There was never a grand design thought up and consistently pursued. In the late nineteenth century an eminent historian, John Seeley remarked that Britain had acquired its empire 'in a fit of absence of mind'. What he was suggesting was that Britain as a nation has not deliberately planned to create an empire. No British government had ever drafted a blueprint.

What tended to happen was that individuals and groups chose to travel and settle in distant parts of the world. No one motive impelled them all. Their reasons were various. Some were looking to make themselves rich by commercially exploiting the labour and resources of the lands they came to; others simply wished to make a better life for themselves and their families in a new land. Some were inspired by a desire to convert the native peoples to the Christian faith; such missionaries were often clergymen, including priests and nuns, who went as teachers, doctors or nurses. Others, not necessarily driven by religious belief, came out of a sense of duty; they set themselves the task of training the local peoples in the arts of government, law and administration. Little of this was government led. Where the government did become involved was as protector of the pioneers. British settlers were often in hostile regions and appealed to the government back home for help. This was usually provided in the form of military protection. British armies were stationed at strategic points around the empire.

As her empire expanded much of Britain's imperial struggle was the commercial pursuit of the commodities to satisfy the tastes and appetites of Europe. There is a striking passage in Margaret Thatcher's memoirs where she recalls how as a young girl helping her father in his grocer's shop she was fascinated by 'the great complex romance of international trade which recruited people all over the world to ensure that a family in [Britain] could have on its table rice from India, coffee from Kenya, sugar from the West Indies and spices from five continents'.

While it is convenient to think of one great united British empire, it was never quite that, except perhaps in people's imagination. The British empire was never one thing, never even one idea. It was as various in meaning as the parts which composed it. In reality it was always a fragmented affair with the differences between the areas as important as anything which united them. There were critical moments, of course, when the parts did act together, as in the two world wars when Britain was able to call on her dominions and colonies. The contribution to the struggles of 1914–18 and 1939–45 made on Britain's behalf by the Australians, New Zealanders, South Africans, West Indians and Indians was magnificent and legendary. Yet this did not indicate any great wish for a closer political bond or collective identity. Indeed, it was the wars that hastened the end of the empire and the emergence of independent states.

The imperial idea

British imperialism was an extraordinary compound of heroism, exploitation, religious zeal, dedication, selfless service, and fanaticism. Fuelled sometimes by a patronizing sense of racial superiority, at others by a desire to get rich quick at others' expense, the imperial motive also sprang from a profound sense of the need to serve the oppressed and the hungry. Many schools of the Victorian era had mottoes in Latin or English which extolled the virtues of commitment. 'Life is service' was typical of such sentiments. A central value taught in the public schools of the late Victorian and Edwardian periods was the duty to serve the empire. It was no empty message. The administrators and district commissioners who laboured in the searing heat of India, the humid jungles of Malaya, or the malarial swamps of tropical Africa were often young men barely out of their teens whose school days had inculcated in them the notion that service in the empire was both a privilege and a duty. Neville Chamberlain, later to be a British Prime Minister, was sent at the age of 21 to run a sisal exporting business in South America. He said he went out in trepidation but with a conviction that he was answering the call of duty.

In Britain, from the beginning, there were opponents of empire who said that, whatever the gains made from it by individuals or by the nation, it was a costly distraction which diverted her from her proper domestic concerns. However, there are historians who argue that the enthusiasm for empire was largely a matter of the hype of its day, deliberately stimulated by businessmen trying to sell goods or politicians trying to buy votes, and that in fact the people of Britain were never much taken with it. The picture, they suggest, has been further distorted by pro-imperial historians who have exaggerated how much ordinary Britons were affected by the idea or ideal of empire. The argument is that Britain was an imperial nation but not an imperial society. This distinction is a subtle one, perhaps too subtle for it to be convincing. In the Victorian and Edwardian eras, the high period of empire, the popular songs of the day and the massive circulation and sales of newspapers journals and books with imperial themes at their centre hardly suggests a lack of interest among ordinary Britons.

What was certainly the case is that taking its cue from the opening up of Africa in the 1870s, the commercial world was quick to use colourful imperial imagery in its advertising. Queen Victoria, Britannia, British lions, regimental flags, military insignia and uniforms were prominent on bottles, packets, and wrappings and in newspaper adverts. With an insensitivity that would offend later generations, black faces appeared on tins of shoe polish, and soap manufacturers made teasing claims about their products being able to turn black skin white.

The debate on the empire

The dispute over whether the British empire was a good or bad thing will doubtless go on as long as empire is remembered. There are many, usually those on the left of politics, for whom empire has became a dirty word. They feel guilty that their present comfortable lives may be a product of the wealth Britain gained through its exploitation of the colonies. There are others, usually on the right, who still take pride in the history of the empire, seeing it as the record of the achievements of dedicated men and women who brought the benefits of Western law, medicine, government and technology to the colonies. A further, fascinating perspective is provided by the colonized peoples themselves and their successors. Much of the history of the British empire is now studied from 'the bottom up'; that is to say, scholars are now particularly interested in studying empire as it impacted upon the local peoples. Whereas imperial history was traditionally written by the colonizers, it is now largely written by the colonized. Hence the controversy that surrounds it, as over the debate about how far imperialism is to be blamed for the mistakes made by countries after they became independent.

'Benevolent imperialism'

Defenders of what is now called 'benevolent imperialism' are growing. They have been prompted by the fact that so many of the ex-colonies of Africa have sadly failed to develop as successful modern states. Questioners asked whether it might not have been better for the colonies to have remained in a co-operative relationship with their former rulers until they had overcome the political and economic teething problems involved in creating a new nation. Liberal imperialism worked better than did the independent nation states left to fend for themselves in a hostile world economic climate.

However, there is also the argument that while imperialism might have often been benevolent it was never genuinely egalitarian. Empires may bring people together, but always in a power relationship, that is to say, one group wields authority over another. The Caribbean is sometimes quoted as a striking example of the first truly successful modern society that has emerged out of imperialism, a vibrant mix of ethnic and social groups. But, as some West Indian scholars have been quick to point out, Caribbean society is a direct result of past slavery, and, however much one might admire what has been produced, it cannot justify the sufferings that were part of its growth. But while not ideal, perhaps benign imperialism has provided the smoothest transition from servitude to freedom.

Another consideration is that the great majority of the new states on becoming independent chose to adopt a Marxist-based form of planning under which private ownership was forbidden, this at the very time when Marxism was being revealed as a failure in those countries where it had been tried. Here again the

West is not free of blame since it was Western advisers and academics who, after independence, trained African officials and students in the fashionable but unrealistic Marxist economic theories of the day.

In relation to this, an interesting idea has been advanced by Hernando De Soto, the renowned Peruvian economist, who suggests that one of the main explanations of why poor countries are poor is that they have failed to develop a workable notion of private property. Lacking that, they have been unable to develop stable financial and political systems, which has left them prey to crippling corruption and despotism. Most of the ex-colonies in Africa came into this category.

The degrees of suffering

The charge is often made that the British empire caused death and bloodshed in its days of conquest and control. This is tragically and undeniably true. But it is also true that no matter how many lives the British may have taken or disrupted, the toll was tiny compared to the numbers of native peoples who died in their own wars or were slaughtered by their own rulers. It should be stressed that before the Europeans came to Africa it was in no sense a united continent. No political, social or tribal unity truly existed. Nor was it a peaceful continent. Slavery, exploitation and tribal warfare were constant. That, indeed, was one reason for the relative ease of European takeover. Administratively, the intrusion of Britain and the other European powers created consolidation rather than division in Africa. It also gave Africans the notion of statehood.

A disturbing figure that helps to put the British empire's record in perspective is that, according to the calculations of such human rights organizations as Amnesty International, there is more slavery and exploitation in the first decade of the twenty-first century than at any previous time in world history. To take just two examples: Moldova, a part of the former Soviet Union, has an appalling record of female exploitation. Large numbers of women are enslaved and forced into prostitution, sometimes within the country itself, but more often smuggled abroad to serve in the brothels of such cities as Paris and London. In the African state of Niger, 50 per cent of the population live in servitude, the abused chattels of their masters.

The Marxist analysis of empire

An interpretation that for generations dominated thinking about the motives behind imperialism was that of Lenin, the Russian revolutionary. In 1917, he wrote that the European states, Britain most prominently, had colonized Africa for 'the purpose of increasing profits by exporting capital abroad to backward countries'. For Lenin, the European scramble for Africa was the inevitable outcome of the growth of capitalism. He believed that by the middle years of the nineteenth century European capitalism had reached crisis point. The advanced industrial nations had become so profitable that they were producing surplus capital that they could no longer re-invest in their own saturated markets. This led to fierce conflict between them for dwindling financial markets. In desperation, the capitalist nations seized control of the world's undeveloped areas with the intention of exploiting them as regions of cheap investment. This was the driving force that for Lenin explained the rapid partition of Africa after 1870. He went further, claiming that the climax of such capitalist rivalry had come in 1914 with the outbreak of the final great imperialist war.

Lenin created the standard Marxist take on imperialism, but his notions were essentially drawn from J. A. Hobson, an English Liberal who had written a bitter critique of British capitalism in which he had complained that the wealthy classes, instead of putting their money into the relief of poverty in their own country, were seeking to increase their profits by investing in the colonies.

The imperialist phase of capitalism, which allows little place for motivation other than the economic in explaining the European colonization of Africa, remains a source of considerable controversy. There are historians who continue to accept Lenin's interpretation as a convincing one. However, critics of this view have established that the statistics of European investment in Africa do not support Lenin's analysis. Most investment went into North and South America and into the old dominions. Relatively little went into Africa, certainly not enough to explain the scramble between 1870 and 1914. Other factors, including, for example, militarism, religious missionary zeal, national rivalry and the use of colonies as pawns in the game of European diplomacy, must be given as much weight as finance capitalism when interpreting a phenomenon as complex as the European scramble for Africa.

The economics of empire

A commonly held view is that when Britain gave up her empire during the second half of the twentieth century she suffered a serious economic loss. However, the imperial balance sheet reveals that Britain as a nation had paid out more in grants, gifts and loans than ever she got back in profits. Despite the common belief that Britain continually drained the colonies of their resources, the fact is that in the period 1870–1940, Britain on a yearly average took less than 1 per cent of India's net domestic product. Even more significantly, at the end of the war in 1945, Britain, having agreed in 1940 to pay all India's war costs, found herself owing the sub-continent a sum of £1,200 million. She was now the debtor nation. It was the same story with the colonies overall. Britain was in debt to them at the end of the war to the tune of £454 million.

Whatever profits individuals and companies might have made, Britain, overall, was a net loser financially. Yet in the end empire was abandoned not because it was making too little but because it was costing too much. The clear proof of this was the surrender of India. Although ideals were involved – from its foundation early in the twentieth century the Labour Party had pledged itself to Indian independence as a moral cause – the fundamental reason why Britain ceased to be an imperial power was because it could no longer afford to remain one. Bankrupt after the war and heavily reliant on the USA for financial aid, Britain could not realistically continue funding the defence and economic needs of the colonies. Moreover, the spirit of the times was all against imperialism. Two world wars had been fought for the principles of freedom and self-determination. Imperialism had become an indefensible idea and a loaded word.

The legacy

In the Monty Python film, *The Life of Brian*, an immortal question is posed: 'What did the Romans ever do for us?' It is easy to substitute 'British' for 'Romans' and ask the same question. Among the obvious suggestions of what, at its best, British imperialism offered might be: the concept of civil society, efficient administration, democracy, the development of transport and communications, the eradication of disease, education, and the administration of justice. But it has also been said that in addition Britain left other less grand but no less enduring legacies. These were scouting and team sports. The scout movement is still going strong a century after its foundation by Lord Baden Powell, one of the English heroes of the Boer War. With its sister organization, the Girl Guides, it has brought enjoyment and purpose into the lives of millions of young people of every class and race worldwide. It proved remarkably adept at retaining the imperial love of adventure and respect for duty while incorporating more modern pursuits and values.

The role of sport

One of history's great puzzles is how Britain, a land of overcast skies and drizzle, came to invent cricket, a game that needs sunshine and light. It was the empire that provided these. Cricket was played everywhere in the empire; it was the universal legacy. And since cricket is not a game but a way of life, it helped to give identity to the dominions and colonies. This explains the passion with which it was played in the sub-continent, Australia and the West Indies. Beating England at cricket was not just a pleasure, it was a national requirement, a way of asserting the young nation's sense of its self-worth.

Nowhere was this more evident than in the fierce rivalry between England and Australia. So intense was this when the English team sailed off to contest the 1932–3 test series in Australia, the *Spectator* magazine with only a hint at parody likened the emotions felt by the nation to those experienced when the British war fleet had left harbour in 1914. The team's ship set out 'freighted with the prayers and hopes and anxieties of the whole English people.'

The matches that followed produced the most controversial series in cricket history. Under the captaincy of Douglas Jardine, the type of aloof English gentleman whom the Australians despised, England adopted 'bodyline' tactics. In order to restrict the scoring shots of the young Australian Don Bradman, the most prolific batsman in the history of the game, the English pace attack bowled consistently short-pitched deliveries on or outside leg stump to a packed on-side field. It was technically within the laws but it broke the spirit of the game. A number of Australian batsmen were struck painfully on the body and even the head. Accusations were made that this 'wasn't cricket'. The row spilled over into politics; angry diplomatic notes were exchanged. England duly won the series, but the Australian side and people felt they had been cheated by a team that had been instructed to put them in their place.

When did the empire end?

Dating the end of empire is an interesting exercise. There are some obvious contenders: 1931, when the Commonwealth was created; 1947, which witnessed the independence of India, and 1956, which saw the abortive Suez venture. But arguably the irreversible moment was none of these but 1973, the year Britain joined the European Common Market. Although at the time of entry, Britain tried to negotiate to retain her special trading links with many of the Commonwealth countries, her decision to join the EEC meant that she turned her back on her old allies and partners. With this decision disappeared the last chance that the old empire or new Commonwealth could be turned into the world's first truly egalitarian, multi-racial, multi-cultural, worldwide economic block. The decision was made in a strange atmosphere of post-imperial apathy and fear. Britain seemed resigned to the fact she was a declining economic force whose only chance of survival was as a member of a protectionist European union. Ironically it was the Conservative Party, which had reformed itself as the party of empire 100 years earlier, that took the fateful decision to abandon the last links with empire. Hugh Gaitskell, the leader of the Labour Party, which initially strongly opposed Britain's European entry, warned that Britain was about to write off 1,000 years of her history.

Conclusion

It is not easy to give a final verdict on the British empire. Its detractors point to the racism and exploitation that accompanied empire building. They refer to the profiteers and racketeers who made their piles at the expense of whole tribes and peoples. Its supporters will stress the economic, social, educational and medical advances that were introduced to peoples who would not have acquired them but for their contact with the colonizers.

Some scholars have argued that empire has been the means by which progress has been made and that it is bad history as well as sentimentality to assume that progress could have come another way. Perhaps it is an indulgence of the liberal conscience to presume that a later generation, detached from the realities of times past, should criticize or apologize for a process that, whatever its particular failings, was in its broadest sweep a force for good.

time line

This time line provides the key dates mentioned in this book.

1494	Spain and Portugal divided the New World between them
1497	John Cabot explored the coast of North America
1509–47	Reign of Henry VIII
1558–1603	Reign of Elizabeth I
1562	John Hawkins led a fleet of five ships to the west coast of Africa
1567	John Hawkins' third slaving expedition
1576–8	Martin Frobisher reached Frobisher Bay and Baffin Island
1577–80	Francis Drake sailed round the world
1585	Walter Raleigh led settlers to Roanoke Island
1587	John White landed in Virginia
1588	Spanish Armada attempted to invade England
1599	English merchants set up the English East India Company (EEIC)
1600	Elizabeth I granted a charter to the EEIC
1606	Settlement in Jamestown, Virginia
1608	Captain John Smith arrived in Jamestown
	Mogul Emperor allowed a British ship to land at Surat

1609–11	Henry Hudson's expeditions to look for the northern passage
1618	Sir Walter Raleigh executed
1618–48	Thirty Years War in Europe
1620	*Mayflower* landed at Massachusetts Bay
1622	1,500 people in the colony of Jamestown
1623	British merchants killed by Dutch on the island of Amboyna
1624	Virginia Company wound up
1624–1732	13 colonies that were to form the USA established
1632	Lord Baltimore established American colony for Catholics
1651	The Navigation Act
1652–4	Open war between the Dutch and the English
1655	Jamaica acquired by the English
1663	Carolina founded as a proprietary colony
1670s	Tea first brought to London from China
1673	James Pitt left England to take up an EEIC post in India
1675	EEIC sent £800,000 worth of Indian cloth to Britain in exchange for British manufactured goods
1694	Creation of the Bank of England
1713	Treaty of Utrecht
1720	The South Seas Bubble
1728	James Cook was born on October 27
1757	Robert Clive's victory at Plessey
1759	British forces under Wolfe took Quebec
1768–79	Cook's voyages
1784	First India Act

1788	Britain founded a prison colony on the east coast of Australia
1793	McCartney mission to China
1804	Settlement at Hobart on the island of Tasmania
1807	Abolition of the slave trade
1809	Christian missionaries arrived in New Zealand
1811	British naval force seized Java
1815	Congress of Vienna, end of Napoleonic Wars
1817	First settlements in Victoria
1819	Singapore leased to Britain
1823	Major Robert Bruce discovered tea in Assam
1826	Settlers began developing Western Australia
1830s–40s	Annexation of Sind, Oudh, the Punjab and parts of Burma
1833	India Act
	Britain formally outlawed slavery in the empire
1836	South Australia founded with Adelaide as its key port of entry
1839	Durham Report
	New Zealand Association responsible for 1,200 colonists settling in New Zealand
1839–42	Opium War
1840	Britain claimed sovereignty over the two islands of New Zealand
1841	James Brooke installed as Governor and Rajah of Sarawak
1842	Chinese signed the Treaty of Nanjing
1843	Natal annexed by Britain
1845–72	Series of wars between British forces and Maori warriors
1850	The Don Pacifico Affair

1850s	Discovery of gold in New South Wales and Victoria
1853–6	David Livingstone's first great expedition
1854	The Convention of Bloemfontein
1854–6	Crimean War
1856–60	Opium War
1857–8	The Indian Mutiny
1858	Government of India Act
1859	By this date South Australia, New South Wales, Victoria, Tasmania and Queensland had adopted democratic constitutions
1860	China forced to sign the Beijing Convention
1866–73	David Livingstone's last expedition
1867	British North American Act
1870–1914	The scramble for Africa
1871	Henry Morton Stanley located David Livingstone at Ujiji
1872	Cape Colony and Natal granted self-government
1873	David Livingstone died
1875	Purchase of the Suez Canal shares from Khedive of Egypt
1876	Creation of Queen Victoria as Empress of India
	Disraeli dispatched a British army to the Transvaal
1879	The Zulu War
1879–81	Afghan War
1880–1	First conflict between British and Dutch in South Africa
1881	British defeat by the Dutch at Majuba Hill
1882	Gladstone authorized the annexation of Egypt
1884	London Convention over South Africa

1885	General Gordon killed in the Sudan
	Cecil Rhodes persuaded the British Government to take over Bechuanaland (now Botswana)
1886	Gold discovered in the Transvaal
	Royal Niger Company formed
1889	Cecil Rhodes secured a Charter for his British South Africa Company (BSAC)
1890	Cecil Rhodes became Prime Minister of the Cape
1891–98	Lord Curzon held various posts in the Indian and Foreign Offices
1893	The Ndebele rose against the British
1895	The Jameson Raid
	Joseph Chamberlain became Colonial Secretary
1897	Queen Victoria's diamond jubilee
1898	British Crown Colony of Hong Kong formed
	Battle of Omdurman
1899–1902	Anglo-Boer War
	France signed an agreement recognizing Anglo-Egyptian supremacy in the Sudan
1900	The Crown formally administered Nigeria
	Battle of Spion Kop
1901	Formation of the 'Commonwealth of Australia'
1903	Colonel Francis Younghusband led an expedition into Tibet
	Delhi Durbar held
1907	New Zealand acquired full Dominion status
1910	Viceroy, Lord Curzon left India
	Union of South Africa
1914–18	First World War
1917	Balfour Declaration
1919	Amritsar massacre
1920	Britain took the mandate for Iraq and Palestine
	National Congress of British West Africa

1921	Amir Feisal accepted as King of Iraq Irish Free State created
1924	African National Congress formed
1930	Gandhi led 'Salt protest'
1931	Commonwealth Act
1932	Iraq accepted as a full member of the League of Nations
1932–3	Bodyline controversy in cricket
1935	Second India Act
1939–45	Second World War
1941–5	Japanese occupation in Asia
1942	Gandhi inaugurated the 'Quit India' movement Singapore captured by the Japanese
1945	The British mandate for Palestine renewed under the United Nations
1947	India became independent Partition of India and Pakistan Burma and Ceylon gained independence from Britain
1948	Britain withdrew from Palestine Empire Windrush sailed to the UK Formation of Federation of Malaya Independence for Burma (Myanmar)
1948–66	The Malayan Emergency
1952–9	The Cyprus Emergency
1952–60	The Kenyan Emergency
1954	Withdrawal of the French from Indo-China Communists withdrew from Malaya
1955	Baghdad Pact
1956	Suez crisis Independence for Sudan
1957	Independence for Ghana and Malaya

1960	Harold Macmillan spoke in Africa of 'the winds of change'
	Creation of the Independent Republic of Cyprus
	Independence for Nigeria, Somalia
1961	Independence for Sierra Leone, Tanganyika and Zanzibar (Tanzania) and Kuwait
1962	Independence for Uganda, Jamaica, Trinidad and Tobago
	Commonwealth Immigration Act
1963	Emperor Haile Selassie acted as mediator at the African summit in Addis Ababa
	Independence for Kenya, Seychelles; Singapore, North Borneo and Sarawak formed Malaysia
1963–7	Britain at war in Aden
1964	Independence for Northern Rhodesia (Zambia), Nyasaland (Malawi), and Malta
1968	Independence for Swaziland and Mauritius
1970	Independence for Fiji and Tonga
1971	Independence for Bahrain, Qatar, and Trucial Oman (United Arab Emirates)
1972	East Pakistan declared itself independent of its Western counterpart
	Independence for Ceylon (Sri Lanka)
1973	Britain entered the European Common Market
1974	Independence for Grenada
1978	Independence for Dominica and Ellice Island (Tuvalu)
1979	Sino-British talks on Hong Kong began
	Independence for Gilbert islands (Kiribati), St Lucia, St Vincent and the Grenadines
1980	Independence for Southern Rhodesia (Zimbabwe) and New Hebrides (Vanatu)
1981	Independence for British Honduras (Belize)
1983	Independence for Brunei, St Christopher and Nevis

There are many thousands of readable books on the British empire. It is a theme that seems to attract good writing. The following is a very selective list.

Niall Ferguson's *Empire: How Britain Made the Modern World* (Allen Lane, 2003) has established itself as a lively, informed and beautifully illustrated study. Another colourful text which tackles the big issues is the *Cambridge Illustrated History of the British Empire* edited by P. J. Marshall (CUP, 1996). A large single-volume book tracing the empire across the centuries is Lawrence James' *The Rise and Fall of the British Empire* (Little Brown, 1994). For those interested in reading the first-hand accounts of empire building there is wide-ranging selection in *The British Empire*, edited with linking commentaries by Jane Samson (OUP, 2001). V. G. Kiernan, *European Empires from Conquest to Collapse* (Fontana, 1982) provides an interesting Marxist slant on imperial developments in the nineteenth and twentieth centuries. James/Jan Morris has written a series of colourful and detailed descriptions of the contradictions and paradoxes that made up the empire: *Heavens Command, 1837–1897*; *Pax Britannica, 1897*; *Farewell to Trumpets, 1897–1965* (London, 1979). A sound, reliable study is Trevor Lloyd, *The British Empire* (OUP, 2003).

There are some excellent individual entries on the outstanding men and women of the empire in the multi-volume *Oxford Dictionary of National Biography* (OUP, 2004), available in all major libraries and on the web. Particularly recommended are 'Robert Clive' by Huw Bowen, 'Curzon' by David Gilmour, 'Raffles' by C. M. Turnbull, and 'Rhodes' by Sheila Marks and Stanley Trapido. A work by Dea Birkett, *Mary*

Kingsley, Imperial Adventuress (Macmillan, 1992), looks at the life of an extraordinary woman of the empire.

Huw Bowen, *Elites, Enterprise and the Making of the British Overseas Empire, 1688–1775* is a scholarly but very readable account of the formative imperial developments of the eighteenth century. A splendid short book describing how Britain and the other European powers gave up their empires is M. E Chamberlain, *Decolonization* (Blackwell, 2004). This is a sequel to her equally short and equally valuable *The Scramble for Africa* (Longman, 1990). A detailed work which offers a balanced picture of the slave trade and Britain's part in its growth and overthrow is Hugh Thomas, *The Slave Trade* (Papermac, 1997). An absorbing sidelight on particular aspects of the slave trade is to be found in Clare Anderson, *Convicts in the Indian Ocean: transportation from South Asia to Mauritius, 1815–53* (Macmillan, London, 2000). Bernard Porter, *The Absent-Minded Imperialists* (OUP, 2004) argues that the empire never had the influence on ordinary peoples' lives that is customarily supposed. Vyvyen Brendon, *Children of the Raj* (Weidenfeld & Nicolson, 2005) is the fascinating and moving story of the British children raised in India.

Among the important books which set out to examine the thoughts and motives behind British imperialism are C. Bolt, *Victorian Attitudes to Race* (London, 1971); J. A. Gallagher, *The Decline, Revival and Fall of the British Empire*, (CUP, 1982); R. Hyam and G. Martin, *Reappraisals in British Imperial History* (London, 1975); C. J. Lowe, *The Reluctant Imperialists* (London, 1967); A. P. Thornton, *The Imperial Idea and its Enemies* (London, 1959); R. Robinson and J. Gallagher, *Africa and the Victorians*. Interesting reflections on the empire appear in the work of the West Indian scholar and statesman Eric Williams, *Capitalism and Slavery*, London 1964. The economics of empire is analyzed in P. J. Cain and A. G. Hopkins, *British Imperialism, 1688–2000* (Longman, 2001).

Many of the paradoxes of the British empire can be understood by examining the career of Winston Churchill. Among the hundreds of books on this outstanding figure the liveliest and most readable are: Roy Jenkins, *Churchill* (Macmillan, 2001), Geoffrey Best, *Churchill A Study in Greatness* (Hambledon & London, 2001) and Richard Holmes *In the Footsteps of Churchill* (BBC Books, 2005).

Outstanding novels which, while not laying claim to historical accuracy, nevertheless provide striking and moving impressions of imperial life are Vikram Seth, *A Suitable Boy*, Paul Scott, *The Raj Quartet*, E. M. Forster, *A Passage to India*, John Masters, *Bhowani Junction*. The writings of Rudyard Kipling and Somerset Maugham are still unsurpassed as insights into the colonial mentality. Many of Maugham's witty and moving short stories have the empire as their setting in *Collected Short Stories* (Penguin). Kipling remains a controversial writer. Some continue to regard him a flag-waving imperialist; others see him as a sensitive interpreter of the ambiguities of empire whose poems, for example, show a touching sympathy towards those most directly involved in the pageant of empire, the ordinary serving soldiers and the native peoples.

On a melodic note, it would be worth listening to the music of Edward Elgar to capture the atmosphere of empire in its high days. Although Elgar did not particularly like his music being interpreted as a celebration of empire, it is difficult to detach his works from such association. His most imperially evocative pieces are the stirring Pomp and Circumstance marches and the luscious 1st symphony. It is possible to regard the poignancy of the cello concerto as both a requiem for the fallen of the Great War and an epitaph on the British empire.

Those interested in seeing the artefacts of imperial history would enjoy a visit to the British and Commonwealth Museum in Bristol, UK, where they will find a very accessible collection of visual and aural sources.

index